M000113056

Awakenings: Stories of Body & Consciousness

Edited by Diane Gottlieb

Foreword by Gayle Brandeis

ELJ Editions, Ltd. is committed to publishing works of quality and integrity. In that spirit, we are proud to offer this work of creative nonfiction to our readers; however, the story, the experiences, and the words are the individual authors' alone. The events are portrayed to the best of the individual authors' memory and some names and identifying details have been changed to protect the privacy of the people involved.

ISBN: 978-1-942004-60-8

Library of Congress Control Number: 2023946704

Cover Art: Woman Underwater in Dress (Modified) by Christopher Campbell (https://unsplash.com/photos/Cp-LUHPRpWM)

Cover Design by ELJ Editions, Ltd.

ELJ Editions, Ltd.
P.O. Box 815
Washingtonville, NY 10992
www.elj-editions.com

Praise for *Awakenings: Stories of Body & Consciousness*

"Awakenings is a celebration of the body, the *whole* body. These essays astonish with tales of teeth, arms, hips, gallbladders, lungs, toes and hair. And hearts, too. These are deeply moving stories about how we move through life and make sense of it all. More than anything, this collection celebrates voices. "Speaking out is a revolutionary act," writes Sarita Sidhu. *Awakenings* is a spectacular revolutionary chorus.

> –Ana Maria Spagna, author of *Uplake: Restless Essays of Coming and Going* and *Pushed: Miners, a Merchant, and (Maybe) a Massacre*

There is such beauty and vulnerability in this collection. Such unexpected joy in these writers' explorations of complicated, hard truths. Essay after gorgeous essay of validation and even comfort. "What if your body is glorious now?" Maureen Aitken writes in *The Question Body*. And my whole self answers: YES.

> –Hannah Grieco, editor of *And If That Mockingbird Don't Sing* and *Already Gone*

This fascinating collection of short pieces, as various as human existence, connects mind and body. More importantly it connects our individual selves to others, as we are shown in brief flashes what it is like to inhabit another body and the unique interpretation that each person brings to this experience.

> –Shlomit Fuhrer, MD, Psychiatrist

I was moved to tears by several of the raw and revealing essays in *Awakenings*. This anthology honors what it means to inhabit the human body—especially in moments of immense betrayal. Cheers to the brave contributors for sharing their most personal stories!

> –Debbie Russell, author of *Crossing Fifty-One: Not Quite a Memoir*

Ever since we evolved enough to become conscious of our physical selves, the human body has been 206 different bones of contention. And that has never been more true than today, when the challenges of the body, and the battles over the body, define so much of our discourse. In *Awakenings*, forty-nine writers bear brilliant witness to the perils and promise of the human organism. Speaking from a wide range of identities and experiences, they write of the body in childhood, the body bearing children, body differences, body dysmorphia, the body in intimate or social relation to other bodies, the body aging, and all the shocks the flesh is heir to. They testify to the body violated and the body rightfully reclaimed. Journeying through this book, you will feel yourself intrigued and awakened. These writers show us how we can empower our own embodiment.

    –David Groff, author of *Live in Suspense*

Regardless of your life experience *Awakenings* will expand your consciousness and awaken you to the real triumphs and challenges of being human. Not the sugar-coated version but an honest raw accounting of becoming your true self in a world that doesn't encourage it. Sharing intimate details of our most important relationship, our relationship to ourselves. This collection is a powerful ray of healing light sent out into the world for all who read it.

    –Laura Malfa, Spiritual Coach and Founder of One Heart

These stories cover every aspect of the body, such as hair, teeth, breasts, things you can change, and things you can't. If you've felt betrayed and empowered by your body, sometimes in the same moment, you'll see yourself in this anthology and come away with a greater understanding and acceptance of human nature.

    –Allison Renner, author of *Won't Be By Your Side*

"*Awakenings* is more than an anthology. This collection is an offering, a chorus of voices carefully orchestrated, singing and howling, sometimes in harmony, other moments in acapella or hushed string ensemble. No matter, you'll stay for the entire concert and find yourself forever altered after. The book launches with "The Body Knows" by Alison McGhee, tugging line by line—through meditation, incantation, song. Essay after essay spans body territory from violation to self-acceptance. I'm left with my own body in sway from the voltage of story, tender and profound, each approached with impeccable craft. *Awakenings* is part of a necessary conversation in our world and will linger in my heart."

–Rebecca Evans, author of *Tangled by Blood*, a memoir in verse

If the body could speak, these are the tales it would tell. This moving collection of essays pulls back the curtain on marker moments from living in a body, inside and out. Together these pieces offer insights and collected wisdom that come from exploring a body's journey through pain, healing, size, health and aging.

–Ellen Blum Barish, author of *Seven Springs: A Memoir* and *Views from the Home Office Window: On Motherhood, Family & Life*

The essays in *Awakenings* explore the exquisite pleasure and pain of having a body. Through these narratives, the writers share not only the complexity of their corporeal forms but also the inner workings of their hearts and minds. We see the many ways our bodies can fail or betray us, make us vulnerable or weak, but we also see the glory in our bodies, which can triumph and survive. I felt newly awakened after reading this stunning collection – thankful to be alive and housed inside my own imperfect body.

–Shasta Grant, author of *Gather Us Up and Bring Us Home* and cofounder of Brown Bag Lit

The idea of the body, the object of the body—the culturally policed and commodified incarnations of the body—are stripped of all artifice and laid unapologetically bare in *Awakenings*. From aging and ability to trauma and transformation, each story in this anthology performs a kind of deliverance upon the reader. Through the brave testimonies and honest accounts of some phenomenal writers, we are reacquainted with our estranged forms and invited to empathize with our fellow humans...we are encouraged to live fully inhabited lives.

–Tara Stillions Whitehead, *They More Than Burned*

With subjects ranging from *mikveh* to miscarriage, *Awakenings: Stories of Body & Consciousness* is an honest and intimate collection of personal stories about struggles with physical frailty, shame, abuse, and body image. For many of the authors, recollecting the past through writing becomes a path towards acceptance and healing. As Alison McGhee says, "Body, oh body, she lives inside you but she doesn't always remember, does she?" Reading these essays helps us remember what it means to belong to a body, to cherish and honor the most vulnerable aspects of ourselves.

–Joan Baranow, author of *Reading Szymborska in a Time of Plague*

Table of Contents

WHAT WE DO TO HEAL

Foreword

I recently climbed into a sensory deprivation tank for the first time in nearly forty years.

When I was a teenager, I loved floating because it helped me disassociate from my body. I'd close the hatch of the tank, lean back into the highly saturated salt water that turned me weightless, and let my physical self melt into the darkness. I became what I most longed to be at the time—a being of pure thought, no messy body to drag around. I had been ill for a year as a teenager, in and out of the hospital, and once I went into remission, I pretended to be ill for another year because I didn't know how to be anyone but "the sick girl." I also kept my period hidden from everyone during that year because I wanted to remain a child, didn't want anyone to know I was growing up. My body was a source of confusion and shame and pain—escaping it inside that dark humid tank felt like relief.

All these years later, floating offered the opposite experience. I felt no sense of "deprivation" when I eased into the water and the lights gently dimmed, then turned off completely—just the beautiful opportunity to sink more deeply into my skin. I could feel the tender presence of my body even after the salt swallowed its weight; I could feel each heartbeat, each breath, for the gift it truly was. When I was a teenager, if my arm or foot bumped into the side of the tank, I would curse the rude reminder of my embodiment; this time, if I drifted into the edge, I welcomed the sensation. There's my arm, I thought—how wonderful that it can feel the world around it! There's my foot, zinging with touch! There's my body, my body that's experienced so much over the years—illness and surgery and birth and grief and injury and exhilaration and discomfort and bliss and bliss and pain and bliss—there's my mortal body, which won't always exist. There it is, blessedly alive and awake.

As its title suggests, this breathtaking anthology is full of such awakening, such somatic reunion. "Body, bring her back to herself," invokes Alison

McGhee in "The Body Knows," the opening piece of the collection, and indeed, in essay after essay, we find writers coming back to their bodies, and finding new senses of safety, of gratitude, of forgiveness within their own flesh, sometimes after years of illness or disability or trauma. "Return to your body," a voice within Amanda Leigh Lichtenstein tells her in "Holy Hour." "It's OK now to return."

The voice of the body, and the urgent need to listen to that voice, thrums throughout this collection. "I have learned to trust my gut," writes DeAnna Beachley in "My body :: in parts," a process that is not always easy in a world that teaches us to experience our bodies from the outside in, to focus on how we look instead of how we feel—a world that tells us our minds and bodies are separate; a world that actively separates us from our bodies. "I couldn't bully away my pain any more than the bullies around me could," writes Barb Mayes Boustead in "Pain's Imposter Syndrome"; "now, I choose to let it speak ... We're still learning to trust each other—me, to trust that my pain is telling the truth, and my body, to trust that I will take the information it gives me to seek relief and assistance and comfort."

The voice of self that issues forth from the body also thrums through these pages. "(M)y mouth is power, magic, bitch, and balm," writes Melody Greenfield in "Lip Service," and the voices in this book are all these things—powerful, magical, healing, bitchy (in the most celebratory and empowering use of the word). "These days, when my doctors use words that obscure," writes Lizz Schumer in "Don't Lie to Me," "I illuminate them. I'm not afraid to drag us all squinting into the sun." The voice that rises from the body, from our embodied truth, the voice that drags us into the sun, can provoke both personal and social change. "Speaking out is a revolutionary act," Sarita Sidhu reminds us in her essay "Shattering the Dark Silence." "This is the path to liberation. This is how hope blooms."

Hope and liberation bloom throughout this anthology, often culminating in hard-won self-love. "(A)s I grow old," writes Marion Dane Bauer in "What I Knew," "as senses and limbs and viscera fail, I love this flesh I was born into in a way I never knew could be possible." In "Men and Their Hands," Claudia Monpere extols, "I want to write love poems to me, to my body. I want to cherish it in spite of a hearing loss and graying hair and arthritis, grateful for all it can do as it ferries me through the years. I used to take comfort in the fact I would be dead someday. Now I take comfort in the fact that I have this dazzling day."

When my hour of floating was up, I stepped out of the dark sensory deprivation tank into the dazzle of light. Gravity anchored my body once again, and I could feel the sweet grounding of my full weight upon this earth. Still, a sense of buoyancy stayed with me for hours; I continued to feel deeply alive, deeply awake and grateful inside my own skin. I felt the same way when I finished reading this book—freshly awake, freshly grateful for my own body and our shared journeys of embodiment. I felt, and feel, so grateful for all these wonderful writers, and for Diane Gottlieb, who so artfully brought them together. May these powerful voices wake you up, in turn—may they buoy and ground you and guide you back to your own tender body and all the stories it holds.

Gayle Brandeis, author of *Drawing Breath: Essays on Writing, the Body, and Loss*

Introduction

Without a doubt, the person who had the greatest impact on my relationship with myself—and my body—was my mother. When I was small and my dear much older sister moved out of the house to get married, I dealt with my grief by eating lots and lots of chocolate and drinking enormous amounts of orange juice. While Mom never came out and directly criticized my shape, I did not believe I mattered much to her until I lost the weight I'd gained—and then some. (I did this in 7th grade by eating only one package of frozen string beans and ketchup every night for dinner.) When I'd come home from a party, the question that awaited me when I walked in the door was not "Did you have fun" but "Were you the prettiest one there?"

The body—my body—became a double-edged sword. By living in my (then thin) body, I risked the advances of boys and men, who, because of biology, or evolution, or God, could not control themselves, and because of the societal and culture norms of the time, did not have to. Alternatively, my body could be my ticket out—of what, I wasn't sure—because one of those same boys might swoop in and rescue me. Neither of these scenarios left me much agency. The only thing in my control was what my body looked like and how much it weighed.

Weight is a heavy word for so many of us. Our bodies' worth—our *human* worth—is placed on many different scales, evaluated according to our body challenges, appearance, sexuality, movement, illnesses. More and more of us are coming together to say "enough" to those judgements, to refuse to take them on as our own. More and more of us are awakening to the gifts that we are and have always been.

Awakenings: Stories of Body & Consciousness, a collection of deeply moving (very) personal essays, charts the journeys of 49 brave contributors who have shared their own body challenges—and triumphs. As editor, I've divided the collection into what feels to me as an organic flow of sections, settling into their own narrative arc. The first section titled "Our Bodies Know" is a tour around the body, a conversation with different body parts, where each claims its due. Lips, teeth, hair, skin, hands, feet, butts, and of course breasts, speak to us and share their wisdom. In "Taking Up Space," we read about size and weight and race and buoyancy. "When It Hurts" takes up pain in its many different forms. The essays in "How We Show Up in the World and How the World Sees Us" explore the critical intersection of who we are and how we are received. There are stories of "Illness as Metaphor," feeling "Separated from the Body," and finding one's way back. "Growing Older" presents different experiences of aging, of looking at the past, appreciation for the present, and hopes for what lies ahead. The final section "What We Do to Heal" is a testament to the spirit streaming through our very flesh and blood, to the strength that lives within all our different bodies, a strength that each contributor has called upon when writing—and sharing—their story.

My mother told me her stories. Often, when I was too young to hear them. Stories of her rubbing her skin raw to rid her body of her freckles. Of living in an orphanage, of being beaten when a leg wound spilled its pus onto her bedsheet. There were other stories, many other stories too. I could not listen at the time. I wish I had.

My deep wish is that you will listen to the voices in *Awakenings*, diverse voices that span across geographies, across race, age, gender, body experience, and any other number of ways one might choose to separate or define them. But it is the contributors' courage and their willingness to put their voices and bodies on the page that connect them more powerfully than any measure that might speak to their difference.

Editing this anthology has been my great honor and joy. I am incredibly proud of this collection and enormously grateful to all the contributors for trusting me with their gorgeous words and for joining me in this celebration of bodies. Thank you, contributors! Thank you—with all my heart and from my every cell.

Thank you also to my dear husband and children, my wonderful friends. Thank you Ariana Den Bleyker for your generosity, for believing in me, and for granting me this amazing opportunity. Thanks to Gayle Brandeis for writing such a powerful foreword and to all who offered their encouragement and advance praise.

Thank you, my kind father and fearless mother, from whom I learned the beauty of imperfection.

Lastly, I thank you readers! I hope this anthology inspires and awakens. I wish you the best and all the love for your one and wonderful body.

Diane Gottlieb
August 3, 2023

Our Bodies Know

The Body Knows

Alison McGhee

Body, oh body, she lives inside you but she doesn't always remember, does she?

You do, though.

You remember for her.

You remind her what she knows, what she has always known.

Throat, you understood.

Understood that words inside needed to be said but couldn't and wouldn't be said because *danger*, because *don't say a word*, because *survival*.

You understood that words held inside, feelings suffocated, would come out eventually but only when *danger* and *survival* were no longer at stake.

You understood an escape valve must be found. You understood *you* were her escape valve. Knew that an imploding girl needed to turn herself inside out until desperation receded, so she could keep going.

Throat, you understood early on that what is now called disordered eating has nothing to do with eating.

Feet, you knew.

Knew you were made not for high heels or delicate sandals or pedicures but for tromping. Miles and miles up and down mountains, running and hiking through woods and deserts and sidewalks and trails.

You knew before she did that through you her mind would finally learn to break free of its fretting, its spiraling, its endless circling.

Knew it would be your tough, rough callouses connecting her to the earth over and over and over that to this day is the surest means to the calm she seeks.

Body, oh body, sometimes she forgets her own power.

Help her remember.

Remember her heart. Heart born glitchy. Heart that sometimes rattles its cage, skips and shimmers along at 200 beats a minute. Hummingbird heart.

Bring back the day they *put her under* and *threaded electrodes* and *isolated the misfires* and *zapped them.*

Bring back the doctor who stood at the foot of the bed, shaking his head and smiling, respectful and impressed.

Do you remember talking to us during the procedure?

Help her remember, heart.

You told us to stop hurting you. There you were, under anesthesia, but still you spoke up and told us to stop setting your heart on fire.

Heart, they set you on fire and you kept on beating.

Mouth, you knew.

Dentists and doctors could find no reason for your swollen gums, sour breath, blisters, and pain. But you knew the reason, mouth. You knew how she feared his touch. You knew she wouldn't act on her own behalf—didn't know how to, not yet—so you took over.

You did what you could for her, and it worked. Because who would want to kiss a mouth in that mutilated state?

To this day, she thanks you for his repulsion.

Cervix, you knew.

Knew how much those dilation rods would hurt. Knew you would cramp and cramp and eventually open. Knew you were helpless against the teen's decision. You were there that day and all the days since. You were with her as the nurse held her hand, witness to both her grief and her relief.

But you also knew, even as the girl lay crying on the table, that your chance would come again, in the future. When she was ready. When she was no longer a teenager.

You knew that birth would be harder for her because of the memory of that day.

You and you alone know why anything in your vicinity—a speculum, a finger, a penis—makes her wary. You know she has coped with that wariness all her life.

Body, oh body, when the world is once again too hard, too rough, she sometimes forgets that the world is also easy. You don't forget, though.

Body, bring her back to herself. Remind her the world is also soft, also gentle. Like that night in the tent, in her t-shirt and shorts, long hair so silky.

How shy she was. How he smiled and held out his hand, after their friends had one by one wiggled into their sleeping bags and been lulled to sleep. How he touched her hair, smoothed it back from her forehead, trailed his fingers over the soft planes of her cheekbones. Soothed her eyes shut and drew her close and closer, in silence. His lips so gentle against hers.

Remind her of that.

Remind her of a long-ago night of soft rain on a canvas tent, how a boy held open the door to another world inside this world, and she followed.

Hands, oh hands.

Oh long fingers. Busy fingers. *Tap tap tapping* fingers.

Hands, did you know before she jumped up that day in first grade to catch the pencil thrown to her that its point would break off and lodge inside your right palm? That it would never work its way out the way they said it would, nor dissolve, nor shrink as the years and decades went by?

Did you know that pencil lead would become her unintentional tattoo?

Did you foresee the thousands and thousands of pages to come, stories scratched out in pencil, then pen, then typewriter, then keyboard?

Hands, those stories have saved her sanity and her life.

She looks now at the tiny blue-black speck in the center of her lifeline, talisman that's been with her through it all.

She lifts you from the keyboard she wrote this on and kisses you.

Lip Service

Melody Greenfield

In the tenth grade, before heading to a New Year's 2000 house party in LA's deep valley—where every strip mall had a run-down donut store, auto body shops were as common as gas stations, and it was always at least ten degrees hotter than anywhere else in Los Angeles—I got wasted with a group of my girlfriends. If I close my eyes, I can feel my way back to that slippery, elusive evening. Before my memories became twisted and jumbled, tucked just out of reach, the alcohol spread warmth from my belly to my fingertips, softening the world's hard edges. With each ounce of liquor I threw back, I likewise threw my problems behind me. As the hours passed, slowly and then all at once, everything mattered—and I remembered—less.

Shot 1:
I forgot I hated my on-again, off-again parents who needed to stop their dizzying dance and break up for good this time cuz all the crazy back and forth was killing me.

Shot 2:
I forgot I hated my bouncing-off- the-walls baby brother for being their favorite when I was the better kid, and he was (at best) a pees-his-pants pain and a pest.

Shot 3:
I forgot I hated my hurl-worthy thighs (no better than pear-shaped Mom's) that jiggled when I shook them and wrinkled when I pinched them. Even at 120 lbs., my body was untamable.

Ten shots and several hours later—as other drunken teens with Solo cups stumbled around me and Jenny from the Block blasted on outdoor speakers—I found my 15-year-old self beside a bowl of Jell-O Jigglers at the party, on grass-stained knees, to the side of the house, where I blew not chunks, not yet, but my first of five strangers. And, just like that, my thighs weren't the only disgusting thing about me.

§

It's been over two decades since that night, and for many of the ensuing years, I continued misusing my body to feel powerful, seen, and in control—repeating this pattern of tipsy sex, of alcohol-fueled promiscuity, until it no longer served me. Until I learned that even two shots may be too many. That my mouth is power, magic, bitch, and balm; that it can sing and whisper, smile and kiss; that it can utter truths and lies, regurgitate information and food; that it can wrap itself around other bodies it has every business—and no business—wrapping itself around. And that, if I want to, sure: I can suck and suck and suck and suck and suck and burn shit to the ground, but also that my lips and I—as easily as we can spurn and hurt and offer services—can offer encouragement, support, and love.

Teeth

Jesse Lee Kercheval

1.   To dream that you have your teeth knocked out, denotes sudden misfortune. Either your business will suffer, or deaths or accidents will come close to you.

Miller's Dream Book

When I was in first grade, I broke my right front tooth. We had been out to dinner, my mother, sister, my dad and I, because my father was teaching a night class and we would meet him for dinner at a nearby Howard Johnson's. For dessert, I'd had a dish of peppermint stick ice cream, one of Ho Jo's 28 Flavors. The ice cream came in a small metal dish and I first ate the bright pink ice cream, placing each striped piece of candy as I came to it on the saucer that held the dish, then, to finish, crunching each piece of candy until it was gone. This helped occupy all the time it seemed to take for grownups— my parents— to finish a meal, which in my mother's case included smoking a Winston. She smoked. I chewed.

Then, as we walked along the sidewalk back to our car, I tripped. In those days, my feet were encased in brown lace-up Oxfords designed to correct my flat feet and it was those feet that brought me down. I tripped on nothing, on air, on my own wandering toes. My tooth hit the concrete.

I can still feel it. Then my mother wrapped what was left of the tooth in her handkerchief, hoping it could be saved.

It could not.

Instead, I got an ugly yellow temporary cap, smeared with gray glue and a bit of my blood. And went back to school with my lips firmly closed over it, refusing to smile. Even for my school photo.

2.

To dream of white teeth means health.

Lunar Dream Book

My father's teeth were white and straight. He died at 65, after years with a failing heart. After the funeral, I went to our family dentist to have my teeth cleaned and he told me how sorry he was to hear about my father. I nodded, all I could do since my mouth was filled by his fingers.

"He had perfect teeth," he said. "Not a cavity. Not a filling." I realized he was crying. "I can't believe he's dead."

But he was.

His tombstone at Arlington National Cemetery looks like a front tooth.

3.

To dream of rotten teeth - trouble with health caused by excessive voltage . . . disease threatens you or your loved ones.

Miller's Dream Book

My bad luck with front teeth started earlier than that night outside the Howard Johnson's. My front baby teeth came in with no enamel on them. My dad was still a colonel in the army then. The army dentist put silver caps on them.

But here I am with my sister, smiling— sort of—in Santa's lap.

While my mother cooked dinner, I remember sitting listening to the radio, waiting to hear "All I Want For Christmas Is My Two Front Teeth."

4.   To dream of teeth filled or capped, you will recover lost valuables
                                                    after much uneasiness.
                                                        Miller's Dream Book

After I broke my brand new front tooth, I had to wait a long time to get my permanent front cap. The idea was to let my tooth grow to adult size. In the meantime, I could not bite anything with my front teeth. I spent two hot summers with my mother patiently cutting corn off the cob so I could eat it.

Then I got my permanent cap and could eat as many ears of corn as my mother had the patience to shuck and boil.

This is, in the course of time, the third "permanent" cap on that tooth. The first one was always too long—the dentist overestimated how much my other front tooth would grow and picked one a bit too large for me. The second, a replacement, was the right length and I had it for decades. The third, most recent one, was a change to match the color of my remaining real front tooth, whose natural enamel was every year less and less white, more stained by a lifetime of coffee and tea than the fake. Now they look identical.

But it never feels quite the same as the real tooth. If feels like a hand inside a very thick glove. Maybe an oven mitt. Or a metal glove a knight wears for battle.

But I can eat corn on the cob.

I could bite you—if I cared to.

5.   Imperfect teeth is one of the worst dreams. It is full of
                                        mishaps for the dreamer. A loss of
                                    estates, bad health, depressed conditions of
                                    the nervous system for even healthy persons.
                                                        Miller's Dream Book

My mother, who had me when she was 42 and died when she was 65, had terrible osteoporosis. Her bones were nearly transparent on an x-ray. Her teeth crumbled. In the end, she bent to pick up a can of soup and the weight broke her back.

She said having my sister, me, had leeched the calcium from her teeth and bones. But, she said, it had been worth it.

When I was pregnant with my daughter, my first child, I asked my obstetrician if this was true.

"No, your baby does not suck the calcium out of your teeth! That's an old wives' tale." She laughed.

But it's true your baby will take the calcium right out of your bones if you don't get enough in your diet." This was in Wisconsin, the Dairy State.

"So remember," she said, "drink your milk!"

6.   To admire the teeth of the baby in a dream:
                                      symbol of recovery
                                     Miller's Dream Book

When my daughter was a baby, I lived by a book called *What to Expect the First Year* which counted down all the milestones your baby should reach in a given month. In Month Five, it told me, get ready for teething! I did. And then—no teeth. Month Six, Seven. I consulted my pediatrician who told me not to worry. Month Eight, Nine. Even she got worried.

I was also worried my daughter's teeth, when they finally came in, might be like mine and come in with no enamel. But that worry earned me another doctor laugh. She said that was called "rapid decay" and it wasn't hereditary. It was caused by my mother's generation letting their babies sleep with bottles of formula in their mouths. "They didn't know any better," she said.

Then finally—just before my daughter turned a year— she got her first tooth. There it was. No teething pain at all. Just one beautiful white tooth. Then another.

With my son, second born, I was so sure he would follow the same pattern before I noticed, at four months, he had a whole row of teeth.

7.   To dream of rotten teeth: a coming quarrel.
                                          Tsvetkov's Dream Book

Growing up, my sister, two years older than me, was the one with the perfect teeth. They were like my father's—even and the perfect size for her mouth. But her life has been difficult. Now she has no teeth. Or nearly. And because of her difficult life, also no dentures. Last year, for Halloween, she sent me a photo of her with her mouth wide open. She said it was a joke. She said she knew it would make me laugh.

It almost made my heart stop.

I deleted it, pretending I had never seen it.

8.   To dream of white teeth: healthy offspring
                                          Hasse's Dream Book

My children both have beautiful teeth. They both floss and brush and go every six months to have their teeth cleaned. They had braces and remember to wear their retainers. They never met my father. They have not seen my sister in years.

I have never asked them if they dream of teeth.

9.   To dream of silver portends worries and unsatisfied wishes.
                                          The New Family Dreambook

                          To dream of silver predicts honor and wealth.
                                          Medea's Dreambook

When my silver baby teeth finally fell out, the dentist—a civilian one by then—gave me a little silver treasure chest to put them in. I still have it. Though I can see it is plastic with just a coating of silver paint. Inside is one of the silver capped teeth, so tiny it is hard to believe it is a human tooth. I am not sure what happened to the other. Did the Tooth Fairy buy it off me?

Next to my silver front tooth is an even tinier baby tooth from our dachshund, Grendel, that I wrestled out of her mouth before she could swallow it.

Two baby teeth from two baby mammals. Looking at them, I feel myself surrounded by a planet filled with teeth, baby, adult, chewing, talking, smiling. Animals all. Unworried by the symbolic meaning of dreams.

I look at my little tooth, twinkling slightly in my hand, and feel such affection for it.

There you are, I think. You and me, still here after all these years.

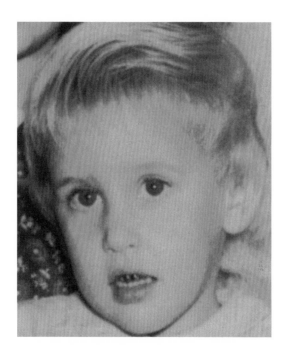

Just Hair

Melissa Ostrom

"**S**hould we layer it?" Jody asks and rests her palms on my twelve-year old's head. She looks like she's conferring a blessing.

Lily's hair is ready—wet, combed, parted. She meets Jody's gaze in the mirror. "A little?"

"Do you want to keep it long?" Jody gives her own long hair a toss. It's the silvered hue of the sun-touched fair.

My daughter nods slowly, admiring that hair.

Where am I? Sitting in the corner, hugging a book, silent. I like that Jody asks Lily what she wants. I do. And my kid relishes deciding for herself. I can tell. We agree: This is Lily's hair.

Clip, clip, clip. Jody circles my girl, her cuts decisive.

Soon Lily looks sleepy, soothed by the process, enjoying being handled by pretty Jody. No flinches, no frowns. "Next time," she murmurs, "I want to put pink or purple in my hair. Or both." She darts a glance my way.

I open my book and keep my expression bland, even though...oh, her beautiful dark hair.

"That'll be fun," Jody says. *Clip, clip, clip.* She pulls Lily's damp strands taut, compares lengths, twinkles a smile my way. "It's just hair."

Clipped strands dapple the floor, dark, damp, curled, like autumn leaves, or tadpoles in a wetland, or too many commas. Or my hair. That could be my hair.

My mother used to save the family's hair clippings for her garden. A strange addition, I once thought, picturing our strands tangling with stems and roots. She took good care of her garden, except during the times she couldn't take care of anything. Those dark-room spells. Her grief had heft, I remember.

I look like my mom, inherited her blue eyes, wide mouth, dusky hair.

Clip, clip, clip. Leaves, commas, unfinished creatures, dark and curling bequests: They rain.

I want to rescue one, hide it in the drawer where I tucked away a lock of Lily's baby hair, fine and fair. I saved it in an envelope, like a message... of tenderness? Yes, but also an acknowledgment of the changes I knew were coming, the growing up, the pulling away.

I think about that letterless letter and my blond baby, my armful of love. Oh, Jody, you are stylish and talented and lucky to touch my daughter so freely. But you're wrong. It is never just hair.

Hair

Eleonora Balsano

Natural Chestnut Brown. The last Christmas before hair matters, your aunt gives you a Barbie in a pink suit, pink heels and a pink briefcase. The following summer she tells your mother off for letting you around her pool topless. Your budding breasts offend her and her trio of blonde, elegantly flat-chested daughters. You learn shame but you don't know yet that stinging feeling of being trapped in an alien body will follow you for decades. Your mother cites caterpillars and butterflies, ugly ducklings and swans, and all you want is to wake up and be something else. Something with wings.

Lightening Spray. The cool girls in school are all blondes. Blondes on TV, blondes on magazines. Blondes on insurance ads and baby formula commercials. The only brunette you spot is promoting a floor cleaner. With your mother's spare change, you buy a bottle of True Blonde spray. You don't know it's just expensive hydrogen peroxide. Ten days later, your hair turns a bright shade of orange. The adults around you yell, what have you done? And you want to yell back, I want to be blonde and pure and popular, but you don't.

Blue Black. Your sophomore year you dye your hair black. Black are your clothes and black is your eyeshadow. Matte black, deep black, black as the graffiti on your school's wall, calling you a *slut* because you slept with a boy, then broke up with him. The adults around you say boys have the right to ask and girls an obligation to deny. Your heart dries out and by the beginning of your senior year, it's the size of a raisin.

Shaved. On the last day of high school, as your classmates fight each other with water pistols, inebriated by the warm air and their imminent freedom, you borrow your neighbor's clippers and bare your head. It is liberating to see your naked skull in the mirror. Your mother says, you will never find a boyfriend if you go out like that, and although you pretend you don't care, her words torment you for weeks. You're as worthy as any man will deem you. Once more, your body feels foreign and inadequate. A cage you inhabit but cannot call home.

Copper Red. You don't fit in with the other girls at university, no matter how hard you try. When you go home you feel your body break into a thousand tiny pieces, a jigsaw no one knows how to solve. You spend many Saturday nights looking at yourself in the mirror, obsessing about your face, your hair, your nose, your eyes. Everything looks too big or too small or simply misplaced, a Cubist portrait. Boys tell you you're too pretty to be smart but when you reject them, they change the narrative. You become a too-smart-to-be-pretty. To break free of clichés, you dye your hair *Copper Red* but it's a matter of days before people seal you in a box again. Women change their hair when they're depressed, they say. They've found an adjective for you, and one that will keep you down and quiet for some time.

Natural Chestnut Brown. Your body pulls an unexpected trick. It doesn't know how to grow a baby. Doctors say you're still young but also that soon you won't be. Your chances of pregnancy decrease every year. They start you on injectable hormones and as you watch bruises appear all over your stomach, blue-green polka dots, estrogens make your hair grow long and thick. Corny commercials make you weep but you are what your mum always hoped you could become. Feminine and pleasant.

Thin Hair. You're a new mother. Clumps of dark hair clog the shower every morning and as your hairline recedes and spiky, new hair replaces the luscious locks of the expectant mum, you don't know who you are anymore. The body you made peace with for nine months is foreign again. Everyone has an opinion: when will you lose the baby weight, why did you stop breastfeeding, let me see your nipples, maybe they aren't as cracked and bleeding as you think. Some days you wish you could tear your body off your soul and be bare again, free from this glove of flesh you can't get used to.

Highlighted Blonde. One, two, three babies. One, two, three ways you find and lose yourself again. Your old clothes don't fit anymore but you don't buy new ones because you are not sure whether there is a way back from where you are now. Some say life is a circle, others swear it's a straight line. You wait until you make up your own mind, and get blond highlights, crossing your fingers that your new hair color won't prevent you from finding a way back to yourself, wherever that is.

Natural Grey. You've been waiting for a while now, but still, you can't find the way, back or forth. Most days you wish there was an adult in the room and you discover that adulthood is a fabrication, like Purgatory, the Tooth Fairy or Santa Claus. A place you are taught to aspire to, generation after generation, but that doesn't really exist. Your body still feels foreign, even more so now that people have stopped looking at it. All you own of you, is your hair. For the first time, you let it be what it wants.

Four Scar and Many Years

Jocelyn Jane Cox

Don't tell me skin is an organ when I know it's just a bag, and liable to break, stretched, as it is, around real organs like the kidney, the liver, the spleen.

Don't tell me skin is an organ when I can see that its decorative paper dotted with freckles and moles, prone to puckers, punctures, and holes.

Don't tell me skin is an organ when it's more like paint, first bubbling then cracking when over-exposed.

Don't tell me skin is an organ when it's flimsy as cellophane, barely protecting what's lies beneath. And don't you dare claim tomato is actually a fruit.

Don't tell me skin is an organ after the damage has already been done. In fact, don't tell me anything, doctor. Just do what you have to do with as much precision as possible to rip out the poison, excise demons, scoop away sins.

Skin's a rind you will puncture, a shirt you will sew, a canvas for unwelcome designs.

I will sit still while you gash and burn.

I will nod when you assure me it will heal.

I wish I could never expose it, or myself, to the sun again.

You've told me it's an organ, the largest of the human body. The scope of the situation, I do understand. Look how much there is, here on the outside: miles of millimeters yet to turn.

I know you are trying to help me fight the forces from without, but what about the forces from within?

Right As Rain

Ezekiel Cork

When I was fifty-nine—and about a year out of a twenty-seven-year marriage—I chose to get a breast reduction for my sixtieth birthday. I despised my breasts, huge farm stock heftiness inherited from my mother.

The surgeon palmed gel samples, and I said, "Smaller." And finally, "Honestly, I want them gone. I don't want them at all."

She sat back in her chair. "We can do that." She grabbed a piece of paper and drew three sketches: a mastectomy with female nipples, one with male nipples, and one with no nipples, only scars.

I pointed to the second drawing. "That one. That's the one I want. I'm not trans but I love the masculine look."

"Then that's what we'll do."

§

"Do you want to be a man?" my ex asked. I knew this conversation about the surgery would be awkward. I'd gone to pick up the dogs that we share custody of and needed to tell her but didn't want to expend energy explaining. It wasn't about her, or us.

"No." I said. "I want to feel comfortable in my body for once in my life."

She is a kind and loving woman who identifies as a lesbian. A word that never described me; I was always gay or queer. I blamed her for refusing to see me. But how can you blame someone for not seeing what you are unwilling to show?

§

When I was a kid, we lived on a maple-lined street in a valley nestled in the foothills of the Rocky Mountains. In the spring when the rain washed the winter from the streets and the air smelled liked angel's breath, I'd stand on the pedals of my stingray and run my fingers through fluorescent green leaves. Water dripped through my hair and down my neck. I was Davey Crockett hiding in the branches with my popgun, hunting game, slaying enemies, and heroically rescuing the captive girl.

The house we lived in had been home to a family who moved away after the mother died. They left things behind in their grief: a curler in the corner of the master bedroom, a plastic army in the dirt below the tree house, one sock in the laundry room, a ruby-red rosary in a kitchen cupboard, and Funk & Wagnall's Encyclopedia Vol. 15: Judg-Long in the bookcase.

On the top floor just off my bedroom was an attic with a tiny window. The room was filled with dusty boxes, a dresser, a chest of boy's clothes, and a full-length mirror propped against the wall. I went there to escape. I'd turn on my Zenith radio, dance and sing to every song, imagining I was the lead singer in a boy band.

I stood in front of the mirror wondering who I was and how to be, searching for a reason for the difference I recognized but couldn't name. I tried on church camp sweatshirts and baggy jeans, a pair of royal blue Speedos that I stuffed a sock into. I flexed my muscles and swam through the air—the butterfly, freestyle and breaststroke. In the attic, I was not a topless girl but a boy dreaming of the girls I wanted like rain.

§

In a drug-hazed stupor after my top surgery, I looked down at the fresh scars and yellow nipple covers and sang, "Hey, it's my birthday." At home, my new girlfriend emptied drains full of blood and tissue even though she's squeamish. She changed the dressings and wrapped the Ace bandage around my chest. With each rotation I would kiss her face and sing "I'll Cover You" from *Rent*.

I lay on the couch for weeks recovering, watching reality television and YouTube videos. Trans men shared their journeys through surgeries, hormones, name changes, even which packers they preferred for everyday use and play. "Babe, do you think you might be trans?" asked my girlfriend.

"No, I just like their stories."

§

When I was twelve, my breasts arrived uninvited. I hated them. Obtrusive and obstructionist, they betrayed the thin and muscled swimmer I was, so I'd strap them in and deny them. I was envious of the boys who had been my friends but started leaving me behind, running shirtless in the streets, the sun rolling over their skin.

I tried dating them, but it felt wrong. My high school boyfriend was a Skoal-ringed back-pocket, Wrangler-wearing, dark-haired, brown-eyed, pickup and gun-racked, bale-buck-muscled, Big Sky-summer-tanned cowboy. I wanted to be him more than I wanted him.

I danced with that boy in the gymnasium under crepe paper streamers and swirling lights. I watched a girl move across the floor. Two nights later I would kiss her and break his heart.

The girls were right as rain. I was their guy holding doors, carrying their books, and lifting them up, lying beside them on riverbanks, rubbing baby oil into their bronzing shoulders, into ribs and the small of their backs. I squinted to see them shiver and watch goosebumps rise on their skin.

I passed windows, my reflection an eerie combination of my mother and father. I was both and neither.

I was strong, proud of my arms, shoulders and legs, capable and sturdy. I loved when girls ran their fingertips over my skin, their whispers and kisses painfully sweet like a tattoo. But I bound my breasts, held them from touch and gaze.

§

After my surgery, with the load off my chest, the swimmer returned. My shoulders were broad and muscled, my pecs defined. I started running again, something I hadn't done for years. My body was like a refurbished classic car and I wanted to see what it could do. I took it out for a spin. I did too much too soon and developed a seroma that the surgeon drained with a gigantic needle. I would end up needing reparative surgery.

I had ghost boob sensations. I had a dozen sport bras sitting on my dresser that I wanted to ceremoniously burn but couldn't bring myself to. It felt like tempting fate. Part of me still couldn't believe that it would last. I was afraid they'd grow back.

My girlfriend was attracted to my masculinity. She never hinted that I should tone it down or settle for androgyny. In the spring, I proposed. I also started reading books by trans men and followed as many of them as I could find on social media. They were telling my story. As our wedding approached, I finally said, "I think I'm trans." I wanted to give her the choice to opt out. She hadn't signed up for this. She kissed me. "I know."

Alexander Chee wrote, "It isn't just that we fall in love with someone—you each allow yourself new identities with each other, new skins, almost like a cocoon to who you'll be next." This time, I was willing to show her who I was, who I had always been. We were married in a Montana ghost town on a gorgeous October day.

I threw the bras away. That December I started "T." My ex who is a registered nurse gave me my first shot. She had never wanted to be with a man. Still, she loved me and would support me through this journey.

Second puberty began in earnest; the zits, "bottom growth," and sex drive. I was constantly grabbing my wife's makeup mirror, flipping it to the magnifying side, looking for new hair follicles on my face and chest. I searched my hairline to make sure it was still intact. My voice started to crack and one day dropped. Six months in, I had a visible beard and shadow 'stache. The veins in my arms stood out. I'd always been muscular but they came in sharper. My mother started to fade from my features and my father who had passed was alive in my face.

§

I'm sixty-two. For the first time in my life, I love the reflection looking back at me.

I jump into pools, lakes and rivers shirtless. The faint scars on my chest are covered with tufts of hair. My wife tells me that I am handsome. She runs her hand over my chest and down the length of my stomach, right as rain.

Late Bloomer

Jacqueline Doyle

I was flat-chested, a late bloomer. That day I was wearing a short-sleeved red sweater with a collar and a fringed vertical panel with three buttons. Was I wearing a training bra yet? I don't think so. Or maybe I just didn't bother every day, since there wasn't much to train. One of the popular girls was pointing at me and giggling with a friend and I realized that the red sweater was really too small and my soft nipples were visible. I flushed with embarrassment.

I was flat-chested, a late bloomer. I wasn't really conscious of breasts at all until the day the girls laughed at me and I realized I had them, tender and sore, straining against the red sweater I'd outgrown. Was this middle school? I remember the classroom, which had accordion doors that opened into another classroom. Students were standing and milling about, so it must have been before or after class. The din receded, I could hear the faint buzzing of the fluorescent lights overhead. I looked down at the scuffed, green-and-beige tiled floor. The room smelled like chalk dust and boys' sweat and funky athletic shoes. My cheeks burned.

I was flat-chested, a late bloomer. I didn't have much guidance from my mother. Not any really, since she spent all of her time in bed, or chain-smoking in front of the TV, watching soaps like *General Hospital*. She complained about her health. "I just don't have any pep today," she'd say. Or, "I just can't shake this cold." I wasn't the kind of daughter she wanted, someone bouncy and popular with a lot of dates. Instead I read books all the time. Why didn't she care what I wore or notice the too-tight red sweater, my budding nipples?

I was flat-chested, a late bloomer who didn't give birth until I was in my thirties. When I breast-fed my son, my breasts swelled to the largest they've ever been. I found it inconvenient. It seemed I was always bumping into them when I reached an arm out for something, or they were always colliding with things. It hurt when the milk first came in, but even the pain felt sensual, and nursing was deeply erotic. I dozed during the rhythmic sucking, awash with pleasure, inhaling the pungent scent of sour milk, which ran in rivulets down my body and soaked the sheets on our futon. I cried inconsolably when I weaned him. My breasts deflated, like balloons emptied of air.

I was flat-chested, a late bloomer, but I never really minded, growing up in the era of anorexic models like Twiggy. My aunt, who came of age watching Marilyn Monroe and Jayne Mansfield in dark movie theaters where boys tried to cop a feel, wore padded bras and talked about getting a boob job. I've always felt my breasts were just fine, and my lovers seemed to feel that way too. "They're an octave apart," one lover said, thumb on one nipple, pinky on the other, as if he were playing the piano. "More than a mouthful is wasted," another said. I don't remember the subject ever coming up with my husband. (Though come to think of it, when he almost cheated on me, the woman had very large breasts. He said she kept bringing them to his attention, leaning over him from behind at work, nudging him to look down her cleavage. I minded the near-infidelity, a lot, but I never envied her breasts. I found it somewhat ridiculous, the way she was always thrusting them at men. I thought he should have better taste.)

Old women's breasts tend to sag, but when you're flat-chested they don't. I look at myself in the bathroom mirror as the fragrant clouds of steam dissipate after my shower. Age hasn't been kind to my body, wrinkled and puckered, afflicted with dull aches here, twinges of pain there, but I still like my breasts, like white peonies, blooming.

Upside to Gravity

Kim Steutermann Rogers

Sixth grade. I'm one year away from getting my ears pierced. Four years away from starting my menstrual cycle. Boys are starting to call, and I'm not sure why. The bell rings, and he stalks over to where I'm sitting at my desk, runs his hand down my back. His body perspires anger, and he opens his mouth to bellow, "Hey, how come you ain't got no tits?"

I feel every one of my classmates' eyes turn to me, then to my flat chest on which an oversized green four-leaf clover is embroidered on a blue-and-white striped knit top.

I creep home alone, tears rivering my face, shame hungering inside me. It felt like he'd broken every bone in my body with his bare words as if he were cracking a Thanksgiving turkey wishbone.

At the close of another school day, my bully follows me out the front door and targets a half-eaten taffy apple at me. It splats the side of my head. This time, I go to the principal's office and report what's happened to a woman at the front desk. She tells me to go home and wash my hair.

§

According to the Centers for Disease Control and Prevention, bullying is a public health issue. The CDC defines bullying as any unwanted aggressive behavior(s) by another youth or group of youths, who are not siblings or current dating partners, involving an observed or perceived power imbalance. These behaviors are likely to be repeated. Bullying can take many forms that fall under three categories: physical (hitting, kicking, punching, spitting, tripping, pushing), emotional (teasing, name calling, inappropriate sexual comments, or verbal or written threats), and social (excluding someone, spreading rumors, making embarrassing comments).[1]

§

A few days before I start junior high, my mom takes me to the local department store to purchase my first training bra. My breasts aren't budding, but Mom knows I'll have to change into gym clothes for P.E., and she doesn't want me to be the only one uncovered. I know the sales lady can see through the charade. As she tilts her head back and peers at my chest through the glasses perched on the end of her nose, I feel my bully is back in the dressing room with me, breaking another bone.

§

According to CDC research, the highest rate of bullying occurs in middle school.[2] Bullying accounts for one of the most highly reported discipline problems in public schools. It's not uncommon for students to skip school because they feel unsafe at school or on their way to and from school.

§

By the end of high school, I'd barely graduated to a B cup bra. Well, not quite. Maybe on my left side but not my right. But that wasn't the worst of it. The worst was that my boobs were adolescent perky. Five-feet, ten-inches tall by the age of 18, I could carry bigger boobs. My mom tried to tell me my boobs were small because I was so tall; my skin stretched over more of my body. But small's one thing; adolescent perky made me feel pre-pubescent, not womanly.

I'm almost embarrassed to admit that I wasn't felt up until I was in college. It was a mere brush with sexuality yet felt like an electric shock, like someone had broken the feeble lock on my diary and read it over the school loudspeaker. And I heard, "Hey, how come you ain't got no tits?"

§

Bullying can result in physical injury, social and emotional distress, self-harm, and even death. It also increases the risk for depression, anxiety, sleep difficulties, lower academic achievement, and dropping out of school.[3] Some children deal with bullying by internalizing it. Others externalize it—turning from victim into bully.[4] Suicide is the third-leading cause of death of children under the age of fourteen, and it has a strong connection with bullying. Over the past three decades, suicides of school-aged children have grown by over 50%, with an increase of 25% just in the last decade. [5]

§

Apart from the woman in the principal's office, I didn't tell anyone about my bully. He was my secret. My shame.

§

When I met Eric, he said he was a leg man. Good thing: I have legs that don't stop, legs that go on forever, legs that wrap around a man. At 25, I married Eric and placed my boobs in his hands, my still adolescent perky B cup boobs. He said a teacup full was just fine with him.

§

Once, on a canoe trip with my best friend and her two adolescent daughters, I felt well-endowed.

We shared a motel room and spent the entire weekend changing from pajamas to shorts and T-shirts to go to breakfast to swimsuits to go canoeing to towels to head to the shower to jeans for dinner and back to pajamas for bed. Every time I slipped off my clothes, I felt adolescent eyes peeking at my naked body. Finally, one said, "Kim, you've got big boobs."

I looked around the room: One petite, late-blooming 12-year-old; one dying-to-bud-and-bud-big 10-year-old; and one deflated and cockled 40-some-year-old mother of two.

My best friend laughed so loud she set off a chorus of bullfrogs in the river.

Still, my boobs were perky.

I know. I know. Perky means you haven't had children and watched your boobs inflate only to plummet like sunny-side up eggs sliding to the bottom of a skillet tilted on its side. Perky means gravity hasn't taken over and your boobs reside belly-button high. But *adolescent* perky means Lolita-like boobs. *Adolescent* perky are like underripe fruit. My *adolescent* perky boobs reminded me of baby birds craning their necks skyward for the worm their mother dangled.

§

There's a growing awareness these days regarding bullying—its frequency, its repercussions, how to stop it. According to StopBullying.gov, a federal government website managed by the U.S. Department of Health and Human Services, research shows that when adults respond quickly and consistently to bullying behavior they send the message that it is not acceptable.[6] Over time, the bullying can stop. The other thing parents, school staff, and other adults in the community can do to help prevent bullying is to encourage kids to talk about it, to establish and enforce rules and polices that clearly describe how students are expected to treat each other, and to create a community-wide bullying prevention strategy.

§

At thirty-nine, I got new boobs. I like to think I didn't have to pay for them; however, the truth is I paid for them back in sixth grade with humiliation instead of cash.

One day after showering as I was drying off, I noticed my boobs in the mirror. Something about them was different. I stood up straight and took a full-frontal view of my chest. I turned to one side. Then, the other. Back to the front. Yep, they had changed. They looked like they had some weight to them now. They looked like they might fill a "B" cup bra. They looked like they might actually need a bra to *lift* them. Gently, I lifted one and let it drop, and then lifted the other and let it drop. And they did—drop. Nature had finally given me what no plastic surgeon could: Gravity. Like a pair of succulent piquant mangoes heavy on a branch, my boobs had flowered into womanhood.

It may have taken twenty-six years for the echoes of my bully's words and taunts to fade, but I like to think it really started one late afternoon that sixth grade year when he stalked me to the school supply closet, his hulking body silhouetted by a window in the closet door, now closed. I summoned strength from who knows where and charged. I don't remember my bully's name, but I can still picture the look of pain on his face when I slammed his back against the door handle. Then, I ran back to our classroom and slid into my seat, got back to my schoolwork. The next year, I went to one school and my bully to another.

Now as I stood in front of the mirror, a slow smile crept across my face, and I threw my shoulders back. Answering the phantom from childhood, "Because I'm a woman. I've got breasts."

Resources:

1. https://www.cdc.gov/violenceprevention/youthviolence/
   bullyingresearch/fastfact.html

2. https://www.cdc.gov/violenceprevention/youthviolence/
   bullyingresearch/fastfact.html

3. https://www.cdc.gov/violenceprevention/youthviolence/
   bullyingresearch/fastfact.html

4. https://scholarship.shu.edu/cgi/viewcontent.
   cgi?article=1946&context=student_scholarship

5. https://scholarship.shu.edu/cgi/viewcontent.
   cgi?article=1946&context=student_scholarship

6. https://www.stopbullying.gov

Perfect

Maggie Pahos

When I stand, my left leg is slightly bent, to compensate for my right leg's shortness, my hips askew. I was born breech, under five pounds. When the nurses tried to get my footprints on a pad of paper for my parents to take home, my feet shot back toward me, and I inked my own face instead. I came into the world all wrong—butt first, feet to face, folded in half. And that was how I made Lauren Beth Pahos a mother. I was backwards and inky and far too small, but my mom was completely in love.

"Everyone was afraid to hold you," she used to tell me. "Afraid they would break you."

But my mom was never afraid of me. She—who smelled like mint gum and cigarette smoke, who drew hearts on the napkins in my homemade lunches, whose angry, coal-hot whisper I can still hear. She loved my brother and sister and me as though she might never get another chance to. She mothered us as though tomorrow she'd be gone.

"I would have held you forever," my mom said to me. "To me, you were perfect."

§

I'm four the first time my mom is diagnosed with breast cancer. My mom is thirty-five. Lainie is three, Willie a newborn. I will remember almost nothing about this time except making a video for her that my dad will bring to the hospital. Lainie and I spin around the orange rug in our living room, creating a circle out of our bouncing selves. We make silly faces, jump up and down as my dad records us on the video camera.

I remember being dizzy. I remember laughing. I remember she smelled like calla lilies when she came home from the hospital. That smell still makes me queasy. The odor of bandages and sickness—of sterility, of medicine, of running in circles until I couldn't see.

§

Every memory of my mom's body includes the scar. Radiation, chemotherapy, a single mastectomy. The scar from breast reconstruction surgery sliced across her back in a deep purple line, a reminder that peeked from swimsuits, a shadow from another life, from a time I could barely remember. Sometimes, while my mom stood in her bathroom drying her hair in her bra and underwear, she'd let me run my finger over the scar, the dark ridge, a dry crack in her soft skin, a fissure in the landscape, her body perfect and then not.

§

In the summers, our family piles into an RV and visits different parts of the country, so we can "keep you close" my mom says in the voice she only uses for dogs and for us, her "love voice" we call it, and we make her say things in the high-pitched, adoring voice, things like "Bowflex" and "Frosted Flakes" and "parking ticket" because we find it hilarious. On an RV trip when I'm seventeen, we stop at Kohl's. We're always stopping at Kohl's for the continuous sales.

"I don't understand how they stay in business," my dad says every time my mom tells him how much we got for how little.

"Because of our family," I think.

We park in the adjoining lot where there is enough space for the RV. The four of us trudge to the store in the heat while my dad stays behind to plot the day's route. While my mom helps Willie look for new school shoes, I want to try on bras. I find the junior's section and pull colorful ones from the rack. I meander to the women's section and pull more, sophisticated ones with lace and underwire, little stitched flowers. Following the signs to the changing rooms, I hustle my goods inside, lock the door.

I take one bra off and try on another, another, another. I make a pile for discards and a pile for keepers, the bras that make the curves of my breasts look full and even, that don't scratch, that are soft and lovely. I look at myself from the front, from behind, at my butt that my mom calls "apple cheeks." I try on the bras with my hair up and with my hair down.

When I'm done, I get dressed, take my keepers, and leave the dressing room for the checkout. I'm sure that's where my siblings and mom will go too. And then I see my mom. She is running toward me, her face pinched. I stop where I am. She grabs my wrist in one hand, my keepers in the other.

"Where have you been?" she yells. "We were about to call the cops!"

"In the dressing room," I say, my face growing hot. My heart is pounding. "What's wrong?"

"We've been looking for you for a half hour," my mom says. "Didn't you hear your name on the loudspeaker?"

I hadn't heard my name. There was staticky pop music in the dressing room. If I'd heard my name, of course I would have come out. My mom throws my keepers on a checkout counter, says to the clerk, voice cheery, "We found her. Thank you for your help, so sorry about that." Instead of buying my bras, she pulls me to the door, out into the hot parking lot. My family is standing there, my brother and sister with a Kohl's bag between them, my dad with his arms crossed. My dad, trying to cut the tension, says dramatically, "I walked all the way over here in my flip flops!" though he's wearing multi-strapped Velcro Tevas, and my brother, sister, and I die with laughter.

For years, the three of us will quote this to each other: "I walked all the way over here in my flip flops!" But each time we do, I feel my stomach brace, hoping no one will bring up the bras, the way I admired myself all afternoon, the reason my mom almost had to call the cops—because I was too vain, too in awe of my own body to care about anyone else.

It is safer to hate yourself, I take it all to mean, to distance yourself from yourself. How conceited to love how you look. How selfish to feel alive in your own skin.

§

I'm standing with my mom in her bathroom. I'm twenty-two, a fresh college graduate. Her cancer has come back—hormone therapy, radiation, chemotherapy. Three years after the re-diagnosis, she's on hospice. There's nothing left to do.

But that doesn't stop us from going to Walgreens to pick up her prescriptions, and before we do, I help her put on her fake eyelashes. Though my hands are clumsy, not right for the job, I'll do anything she asks of me, anything at all. I take a deep breath, concentrate. My mom's eye quivers beneath my finger, and with my own eyes squinted, my hands steady, I press the lash against the lid. It sticks. I guide the rest of the lash across, press so it stays.

"Did you get it?" my mom asks, blinking. She opens her eyes.

"I think so. What do you think?"

My mom leans toward the mirror.

"Looks good," she says. "Now, the next one."

When I'm finished, my mom stands back and takes her wig off the counter. She places it on her head, adjusts the wig, clips her hair to get it out of her eyes.

"I'm all smoke and mirrors," she says, talking to my reflection. "Most women are, but I *really* am. You could look at me and never know."

§

An hour later, my mom and I stand in front of Walgreens. Underneath her big jacket, her body has shrunk to nothing. Her fingertips are yellow from her failing liver. A bruise blooms on her knee from a middle-of-the-night fall. But from a distance, we look like any regular, healthy pair on a Wednesday afternoon. Her wig is straight and un-mussed. Her eyelashes have stayed on, her lipstick too. See? I'll want to tell my seventeen-year-old self. It isn't vain, but rebellious, to feel alive in your own skin. It's an act of survival to show the world who you know yourself to be.

In the parking lot, my mom and I are talking about who will take care of me when she's gone. We're both crying, and she pulls me into her. What they don't tell you is that grief is a thousand losses, packaged as one. What they don't tell you is your body becomes a carrier ship for them all. My mom's left breast, the one they reconstructed all those years ago, pushes against my chest, firm and stable. The right one has deflated along with the rest of her body. My left leg is bent, to straighten out my hips. We are both uneven, mismatched, intertwined. We are made up and broken down, wet faces to the world.

In seven days, she will be gone. Right now, we are perfect.

Like a Kardashian

Kelli Short Borges

I want to hate Kim K. I really do. I want to hate her for all the reasons some people love her—her over-the-top obsession with appearance, down to the smallest (false) eyelash, her glossy black extensions (recently dyed blonde, her absurdly thick braid reaching the floor like some kind of modern day Rapunzel), her perfectly slicked lips pouting seductively from every magazine at the grocery store, pillowy as clouds, while I stand in line with my pepperoni hot pockets and thin, chapped ones, licking them self-consciously, searching my purse in vain for a stick of half-melted cherry ChapStick.

I want to hate her. I really do. But I can't.

Because of her butt.

Real or fake (it remains debated), KK's butt has become the coveted shape for rear ends. I personally don't care which it is, real or fake, because my own "got-it-from-my-mama" rear looks very much like that of a Kardashian. And that makes it suddenly—for the first time in my life—fashionable.

For as long as I can remember people have commented on my butt because for a semi-thin white girl, it really stands out. As a kid I got nicknamed "bubble butt," and it stuck. My butt has its own zip code, and whatever my address, the zip stays the same. Men comment. Women comment. Little kids comment. My butt has become its own celebrity. When I became pregnant with my first child my butt was as round and full as my stomach. It looked like I was carrying twins, one in front and one behind. Only one would ever be birthed.

My friends teased me in a good-natured way, and I laughed along with them. But I was secretly jealous of girlfriends who looked like they were just "carrying a basketball." Those you "couldn't even tell were pregnant" from behind. Kate Moss was the celebrity of the moment back then, and my butt was as big as her entire body. In shame, I started trying to hide it. Behind long jackets, baggy pants, sweatshirts tied around my waist. No amount of dieting could change my genetic lottery, and eventually I reluctantly accepted the fact: my butt would remain ample.

But then, years later, out of nowhere it seemed, came Kim. Launched by a sex tape, KK suddenly became a household topic of discussion, her butt a star. Many people were appalled at first. How dare she flaunt her abundant rear! Shouldn't she be hiding it under muumuus? Shouldn't she envy other, much smaller, rear ends? Shouldn't she be more like Kate? But Kim stood proud, and soon hers became the rear everyone wanted, the "butt of the moment." And for the first time ever, so did mine.

A few months ago, I was at my local mall, trying on jeans. As I came out to check my back view in the three-way mirror (it looked pretty good!) a group of women in their twenties noticed me and gathered around. "Those are so cute," one said, eyeing me, her own small rear clothed in sleek white Lulu leggings. Then, "How did you get that butt? It's really great." Her friends nodded along.

I wish I could say I didn't care, but I did. Flattered, I thanked them. In that moment, though, looking at those young women, I couldn't help but wonder why there has to be *any* pressure to possess whatever butt is "on trend." Wouldn't it be amazing if we all just embraced our shape, no matter the angle of our curves? Maybe someday, together, we'll get there. I'd like to think that we can.

"Hey, what kind of jeans are those?" one of the women called as I headed toward the register, perfect new jeans in hand. Checking the tag, I told them the brand. As they walked away to find the same pair for themselves, I shouted after them—

"You know, these are designed by the Kardashians."

Bible Cysts

Karen J. Weyant

One day, while I was typing, I glanced over and saw a lump the size of a ping pong ball pushing out from the top of my right wrist.

I wondered what it was—and how long it had been there and I hadn't noticed.

I pressed down on the ball of flesh with my left hand and my fingers made an indent, almost flattening the skin, but when I released my fingers, the ball popped back into place. There was a little tenderness but no real pain.

"It's a ganglion cyst," my physician's assistant said at a checkup a few weeks later. She picked up my wrist and pressed down on my skin. "They used to be called Bible cysts. Women used to take the heavy family Bible and slam it down on them." She paused, "I wouldn't recommend doing that now," as if she thought I was conjuring some type of home treatment in my mind.

Ganglion cysts are fluid filled sacs that most often form on wrists. Causes are unknown, although women seem to have more of these kinds of cysts than men. Most descriptions suggest that these cysts first appear in women between the ages of 20 and 40, although I was 47 when I first noticed the strange bulb spring from my wrist.

My PA told me there was little I could do. "If you drain the fluid, there still is a good chance the cyst will come back." She paused. "Does it bother you?"

I flexed my wrist. "No, not really. But it's not pretty."

She laughed. "Well, it may come and go, and as long as it doesn't hurt, I would leave it alone."

A few weeks later, I noticed a similar cyst growing on my left wrist. This one was the size and shape of a pea pushing its way out to the side, right below the muscles of my thumb.

Another checkup. Same diagnosis. Another ganglion cyst.

So, I had a mismatched set. And on my physician's assistant's advice, I left them alone.

§

In the introduction to her book *Hands: Physical Labor, Class, and Cultural Work,* historian Janet Zandy says simply, "Hands speak. In sign language they do the work of tongue and voice box. In greeting, they iterate multiple meanings. They augment orality. They reveal identity – the long fingers of the pianist, the rough stubby hands of the bricklayer." Zandy's book is an exploration of the stories of working-class people told through their hands. I understand. I came from a working-class family, and when I think of my family's hands, I often think of the cuts and bruises of factory work, the stains of dirt and grease from outside work, and the burns and scrapes of kitchen work. Hands equate with work, and each scar tells the story of that work.

Still now, when I study my own wrists, I think about more than the physical work that marked our lives. I think of the way arthritis crippled so many members of my family.

My grandmother's fingers may once have been long and delicate, but I only remember them as skinny and twisted. My mother's hands swelled so that in the last years of her life she could no longer do the activities she loved the most. My Uncle Richard's hands enlarged into boxing glove mitts. The list could go on and on. Indeed, when I think back to these family members, most of them gone, it's hard for me to remember healthy hands.

It's been three years since the first cyst appeared, and since the initial diagnosis, I watch as both cysts come and go. The one on my left wrist is especially interesting, as there are times it totally disappears. Other times, however, it grows into the size of a golf ball. When it expands, I feel a bit like Frankenstein's monster as depicted in the 1931 black-and-white classic. The bolts in the monster's neck are what most viewers remember, but a closer look at Boris Karloff's monster reveals wrists that are thick, bulging and gangly. The balls on the top of my wrists aren't part of me – they are really some kind of extra part, something like a bolt perhaps, that is helping to hold my body together.

The true cause of ganglion cysts is unknown, but some studies suggest wear and tear of the tendons. Others suggest arthritis as an underlying cause, and because of my family history, that is what worries me the most. I wonder when my fingers will twist into knots. I wonder when my hands will swell beyond recognition. I wonder when they will no longer be mine.

The Feet

Cynthia Wold

They shout, "We're not just carriers! We are everything!" In their lumpy, crooked, bunioned, calloused voice.

The revolution started years ago with the second toe on the right foot. In a moment, standing like a stork in yoga class, bloop! The toe shifted sideways, a bend at the knuckle that wouldn't straighten. It didn't hurt, it just felt weird, like my foot was part of a different body, not mine.

I started exercises, pulled my foot up behind my back, stretched the top/front as well as the bottom/back, and wore shoes that allowed toe separation. All of this may have prevented something (how could I know?), but it didn't make my toe straighten.

So began my enlightenment to the travails of feet that must scream to get attention. Not so for the more glamorous and engaging eyes (windows to the soul), or breasts (food bringers), or legs (propellers to somewhere). Feet become invisible. They're the underneath, the basement floor, the place no one goes without a fetish, unless something is broken, throbbing, getting in the way, or causing trouble elsewhere.

I remember the times my feet screamed for mercy; when I walked in high heeled sandals to and from school, preferring cuteness to comfort; when I flew around restaurants laden with trays; when I stood behind bars for hours telling jokes or listening to sad stories; when I squeezed the square peg of my foot into the round hole of a stylish shoe. And even then, the poor things were given a plaster or a short rest, and then back to the grind, back to their place, underpinning everything.

When I was a child, I saw a movie called *The Inn of The Sixth Happiness*, starring Ingrid Bergman. The protagonist fails to become a missionary in China but is hired in a small village to be the "foot inspector." That was the first time I heard of the practice of "foot binding." Girls were forced to wrap their feet in tight, painful bindings from childhood because small feet were considered more "attractive" to men. The practice had been (and continues to be) banned, but inspectors traveled to remote areas to make sure families complied with the ban. Many did not. At the time I was grateful that we didn't do that here.

Since, I have often thought the practice of wearing the sort of shoes that are considered "attractive" for women is a kind of voluntary foot binding. It is (has been for me) a painful force that inhibits movement, interferes with posture, prevents running, but is considered a requirement for sophisticated fashion.

I used to despair for the future of my daughters when popular culture was encouraging the tallest of spike heels and the pointiest of toes. I would see young people totter about in shoes that could legitimately be called "cruel."

My feet were battered lost girls who broke open my heart. I get them good, sturdy, roomy shoes with metatarsal support, and make sure my babies have a good home. I soak them in warm water, massage them with lavender foot cream, trim and smooth the rough edges. I caress the wrinkled middle toe and cushion the corn that cries if I'm not careful.

This was going to be a story about my body as a whole, but now it is all about the feet, because they have won. They are galloping unicorns in the dark forest; hearing everything, saying nothing, bearing all.

My body :: in parts

DeAnna Beachley

My hair: I had short hair as a girl, I think because it was easier for my mom to spare me the long moments of teasing out knots she faced as a girl. I always wanted long hair, especially after I glimpsed my great grandmother in her white cotton nightgown, unwrapping a braid that looped around her head a couple of times into an iron gray rope that fell below her waist. I started college with super short hair, after a terrible experience with a Toni home perm and an aspiring hairdresser my dad pressured me to see. Before I started coloring my hair, the guy at the garage where I was having a tire plugged, looked at me and said, *I think your gray hairs are very sexy*. Or the older guy at work who tugged on my braids and told me he would have dunked them in the inkwell when he was in school. Or the guy who followed me around Target to tell me, *you have beautiful hair*. I no longer color my hair, which now falls at hip level. My graying crown.

My eyes: *Doe eyes*, *bug eyes*, eyes that mean I'm *full of shit*. Brown eyes = shit eyes, according to a boy on the bus. I wore glasses in 7th grade. My older brother teased me that I looked like Mrs. Beasley (from *Family Affair*), so I stopped wearing them. When I finally had to wear corrective lenses in college, I chose contacts. In the absence of contacts, the house is a fuzzy place of colors and vague shapes.

My ears: Long lobes, shaped the same as my dad's. Like many women of my generation, I have them double pierced. I can wiggle my ears. The first time the man I married nuzzled my ears, our second date, we wandered around a small gallery looking at Impressionist paintings, and he whispered to me he loved how I looked in my dress. We huddled close speaking softly about the paintings. I wore a green checked sundress, the pattern danced like the swaths of blue, red, and yellow of the Renoirs we viewed.

My lips: I do not have full lips; my mouth is small. My mouth is the same as my mom's, set in the same line. Someone once told me, *you look so Little*

House on the Prairie until you open your mouth.

My nose: Shaped like my dad's, but not as large. I have a slight bump on the bridge, and a fibrous papule on the left nostril, but not as large as the one my great grandmother had.

My cheeks: I have a dimple on my left cheek that shows up when I smile. As a girl, I sported freckles on my cheeks in the summer. One guy told me *I love freckles on a woman.* My cheeks flush easily from heat, wine, or embarrassment.

My neck: Long. My older brother used to tease me about being a turtle. And then I got to college and learned about the beauty of a long neck from Parmigianino's painting *Madonna with the long neck* (1535-1540). For years, the voice that emanated from my throat did not seem to be my own. I ugly cried in the bathroom the first time I read a poem of mine in public. In a class on the chakras, my teacher said I had a blocked throat chakra and recommended focusing a blue light on my neck. I sat for fifteen minutes a day for a couple of weeks basking in the blue glow. My neck is now lined with age. Is this like palmistry where you count the lines on your wrist to figure out your age span?

My hands: I can reach an octave and one key on the piano. This made playing Chopin more difficult, too many complex chords. My piano teacher helped me change the fingering so I could play. My hands look nothing like my mom's, who has long, tapered fingers. Aristotle once wrote: *Lines are not written into the hand without reason.* My hands are square since my fingers meet the length of my palm. I learned from a palmistry book I have the teachers square—the cross-like marks that appear below my index fingers. When out in public, I wear 27 rings on my fingers. I stack the rings two or three or five on a finger and thumb. My cousin's daughter asked me once how many rings I wore, and we counted, and then she asked, *is this how many times you've been married?* I told my grandma this story and every time after that, even the last time just a couple of months before she died, she looked at my fingers and laughed.

My boobs: Sagging now. Never large. And yes, I did chant: *I must, I must, I must increase my bust, the bigger the better, the tighter the sweater, the men depend on us.* It didn't work. Looked longingly at the ads for the Mark Eden Bust Developer in the back of the women's magazines my mom received in the mail. My mom always bought me padded bras and bathing suits, so the nipples never showed. After church one Sunday, Mr. Smith (let's say) greeted me and picked up the pendant I wore to look at more closely. As he placed it back down, his hand grazed my left breast. I adopted a new slogan in college: *any more than a mouthful is a waste,* and for a couple of years, I stopped wearing a bra. At work one day, my co-worker's husband peered down my blouse, and said *nice tits.* I started wearing bras again.

My belly: Poochie with age but was always slightly round. A guy once told me that he found that sexy. My belly, my poochie, no scars, no stretch marks from pregnancy. Still smooth, there's just more of it now. I have learned to trust my gut.

My back: I wish I had one photo that my ex-fiancé took. My naked body shrouded in a white sheet, late afternoon sun slatted from the window blinds, creating stripes on my back. A lover, who saw a copy of that photograph in a gallery, told me that he wanted to lay his tongue where the sheet met the lowest part of my exposed back. And yes, he did. My back now noticeably fat where the bra rests.

My hips: I love the Lucille Clifton poem "homage to my hips," a poem that I wish I would have discovered many years sooner than I did. My hips are large, much larger than my belly, even when I was in my 20s. I had to use safety pins to tighten the waist for the pants that fit my hips.

My ass: Dimpled from cellulite. I always had a bubble butt. My mom and all her sisters are similar. We are an array of pears. When shopping for clothes a couple of years ago, a woman looked at me and said, what are you doing in this aisle? I turned and showed her the junk in my trunk.

My legs: What can I say about my sturdy, thick legs? I never had a thigh gap after puberty. My thighs rub together, chafe in the heat, and I never wear corduroy. I have a low center of gravity now and have difficulty standing up from a squatting position. But these legs, these legs, have carried me on trails through canyons and mountains. They have rested in front of magnificent paintings and sculptures. My ankles are not the delicate turned out ankles of dancers or the gleeful lady on *The Swing* in the Fragonard painting. My ankles are the peasant ankles in Millet's *The Gleaners*.

My feet: I have a photo of my older brother and me walking to my first day of kindergarten. You can clearly see that I walked pigeon-toed. Even now when I am tired, my feet naturally turn in. My feet have never been arched like a ballerina's (did I ever want to be a ballerina?). Mostly flat footed, prone to *Plantar Fasciitis,* I keep a golf ball on my bedside table to roll under my feet when they ache. A half size larger than what they settled into for most of my life. Trying to keep the bunions at bay with toe stretchers and regular massage work. Once, during the summer, while at the university library, a man approached and told me that I had beautiful toes, said, *I want to lick your toes.* With a flick of my braid, I walked away.

Taking Up Space

Water

Tania Richard

When I swim, I don't feel my body in the same way I do when I'm on the ground. I don't feel the weight of it. The pain of it. The trauma. The history or the shame.

After I finish my laps, I float on my back just past the shallow end. I lower my legs until I tilt over onto my stomach. As I tilt forward, I stretch out my left arm and point my finger while I bend my right arm and rest it on my hip. I am a superhero ready to take off for flight.

I repeat this move over and until the slow tilt forward feels seamless and natural. As my body rotates, I imagine that my black swimsuit transforms into a bodysuit with a flowing black cape. My goggles turn into a cat eye shaped mask.

I probably look like a weirdo, but I don't care. In the pool, I don't care about anything but the meditative strokes of my freestyle, the resistance of the water as I move against the current with a blue noodle between my legs. I don't care what I look like when I do intermittent water aerobics and jumping jacks in the middle of the pool or balletic stretches on the side.

When I swim, I have a swimmer's body: long, lean, small, pert breasts, flat stomach, taut arms, a space between my legs. When I get out of the pool my body has mass, my breasts are big, my waist is thick and my thighs touch. My arms have contour and muscle, but I think they are big and don't like to show them. My skin is brown.

I have no idea if I am fat or thin. I think I am slightly larger than average sized, but I don't actually know if that's true. I spend most of my time around white women at a distance. I see them in locker rooms or in attendance when I lead a workshop on antiracism. White women tend to make themselves even smaller then. In deference. I don't expect them to, but it happens.

My husband is also a swimmer. On Sundays, we swim in the same time slot. He loves seeing me in a bathing suit. I don't like him seeing me in a bathing suit. I worry he'll get a 360-degree view as opposed to the angles I control in the half light of our bedroom.

In grade school and high school, I thought I was fat. I felt fat. Was I fat? All of my classmates were tiny white girls. I performed in musical theatre, so in my free time I was around tiny white girls who were dancers. That certainly didn't help my sense of self.

In a cheerleading picture from 7th grade, my waist is wider than the other girls, my shoulders more expansive, my thighs and butt thicker. If I grew up around Black girls, I would have seen myself reflected more often than never. But I didn't grow up around Black girls.

In high school, I ate my way, far away, from the white girl ideal. In college, I tried to shrink myself back, with Opti-fast. That loss lasted until I gained the weight back and then some. In my twenties, it was Weight Watchers, then watching the weight come back, then Weight Watchers, then maintenance, then childbearing, then Weight Watchers, again. And always, a steady diet of body shame and confusion resulting in ever present dysmorphia.

Back to the pool. Or really, the locker room. One time a white woman who shared a lane with me passed by and said, "It looks like you're having so much fun just splashing around in there." Her tone had a suggestion of sarcasm, a tinge of judgement. I hear subtext, so I knew she meant, "The pool is meant for real swimmers. And even though you weren't in my way I still don't approve of how you took up space."

I responded with "Ya know, I really am," then flashed an overdone, satisfied smile. My subtext: "I can do whatever the fuck I want and your commentary isn't welcome."

Another time, an old white woman in my water aerobics class floated over to me and said, "You have the most beautiful shape. I want to strangle you." At "strangle" she held her hands apart and squeezed my imaginary neck.

In a moment of weakness and cognitive dissonance, I giggled like a schoolgirl who just received a compliment. I never believe my husband when he says I have a beautiful shape, but a *stranger* said it. Someone who doesn't love me. That's a real-deal compliment. 100% bo-na-fide.

Later, I realized it wasn't a compliment at all. Rather, it was an assault. She told me, a stranger, that she wanted to strangle me. She said that she thought my body was beautiful and because she thought it was beautiful, she wanted to take my breath. I keep a distance from her in class now. I don't look her way.

I abruptly decided to start swimming in June of 2022. I was sitting in the family room feeling irritable, bloated and cramped in our green art deco armchair. I kept shifting my weight, crossing and uncrossing my legs. The rayon and spandex material of my pants overheated my skin. Even though they were loose around my waist, the fact that I could feel the waistband at all made them intolerable.

I'd recently seen a picture of myself that sent me spiraling into regret and self-hatred. In the picture, I am wearing black pants, a green flowing shirt and black mules. I sit on the corner of a table along with two older white men and a young, lithe white woman. They all looked exactly as they did in person, so the picture I saw of myself had to be accurate.

My face was fuller than I thought; my shoulders were more rounded. I'm smiling and look healthy, average for my size. I had gained back every one of the fifteen pounds I'd lost from having Covid and pneumonia—when I was the thinnest I'd ever been.

Once I was out of the woods, I loved the way my cheekbones popped and my collar bones jutted out on Zoom calls or selfies I'd post on social media. At a kid's outdoor birthday party, a mom said that I looked gaunt, her face shadowed with concern. I took it as a compliment. I looked drawn, tired, fragile and weak, but I couldn't conceive that being emaciated wasn't some kind of win.

The picture was proof that I'd come out of a life-threatening illness. I wanted to be grateful that I was physically healthy again, to accept that weight gain was, in fact, a good thing. I needed to find a way to connect to my body that had nothing to do with how it looked. I grabbed my phone, looked up swim times at the YMCA, then announced I was going for a swim.

In the pool, I take on whatever challenge I fancy. Two laps of breaststroke, two freestyle, mid-lane aerobics then freestyle again. Because when I swim, I listen to my inner voice and answer my spirit's every request. Then, out of the pool, I am able to move through the world with skin attached to my bones. I am not defined by what my body looks like. I am not only my body. I am the children that I've carried, the love that I make, my connection to each present moment. In the pool, I point to the future in my superhero stance. And that holds me until I'm back in the water again.

The Light in Him

Aria Dominguez

The fat man runs chubby hands along silver rails as he descends the four steps into the whirlpool. He lowers himself onto the tile bench we all trust is there, even when it is obscured by churning water. Two of the three individuals currently steeping in the hot tub rise with unmistakable looks of disgust. The other has his head tilted back, eyes closed, unaware of the scene unfolding in front of him.

"There are only three people allowed at a time!" snaps the lone woman as she gives him a wide berth, stomps up the stairs. He hadn't seen the sign noting new COVID rules and apologizes, says he will get out and wait his turn.

"Forget it," she growls, grumping off across the white tile floor, as if the mere sight of him ruined her day. As if the sign doesn't also say one should limit their time and exit if others are in queue.

The middle-aged man who had leapt over the edge as if a leper were contaminating his personal spa *could* get back in, now that the woman's departure lowered occupancy to the allowable three. I tell him as much, say I am willing to wait if he hasn't had enough time to soak. He shakes his head, still sneering, jams his feet into cheap plastic soccer slides, and departs.

I am taken aback that grown adults are playing the cooties game like children on a playground. I can still hear kids shouting *Aria has cooties!* as they run away. The more I claimed, *No, I don't have cooties!*, the more it legitimized the idea of cooties, the more it made my denials sound weak and false. What I was really trying to proclaim was, *No, there's nothing wrong with me!* Even if I didn't believe it. Even if I feared they were right.

I shrug, "If you're leaving, I'm getting in then."

I slip into the steaming water, flash a friendly smile at the large man across from me. Usually, I avoid eye contact with men in hot tubs, and would certainly never smile. I found out the hard way that politeness is an invitation to be made a captive audience. That a resting bitch face is as necessary as a swimsuit. But I feel compelled to offset the cruelty I just witnessed. The man's face seems sad, but he returns a smaller version of my smile. Several minutes later, when I turn to shift my other hip to the jet, he still looks glum, and I grin at him again. I try to convey in a moment's glance, *Forget those jerks. I don't have a problem with you.* I want to imagine he understands, because he smiles back a little bigger, gives a tiny nod. Perhaps I just want to make myself feel better. Probably my grain of kindness is nothing against the cruelty piled on the scales of his life.

When I rotate to let the pressurized stream dig into my lumbar region, I am fully facing him. He has shut his eyes, is leaning back, relaxing into the soothing water. His generous man boobs rest on his protruding paunch, one sagging toward each side. His physique reminds me of the Happy Buddha statue my father brought home from his travels. Under the scruffy beard his face looks innocent. Gentle. Sweet.

A phrase pops into my head unbidden: *The god in me sees the god in you.* Some say, *The light in me honors the light in you.* I have always found it cheesy, suspected it's a granola hippie appropriation of Indian culture that's likely not even translated right. But suddenly I see the point. It doesn't even have to be divinity. It could be *The fatty in me sees the fatty in you.* Or *The rejected in me sees the rejected in you.* Even something so basic as *The person in me sees the person in you.* He is a different gender, age, race, height, and size than me, but those are external divisions. Peace between us could come simply from recognizing the same lifelight shines in both our beating hearts.

I am overcome by sadness at how the others looked at him as if he were not even human. As if his more-ness made him lesser.

Not only do people make aesthetic judgements about fat folks—they make moral ones. They look at a slim person and assume health, fabulous willpower, general superiority. It is irrelevant that there are many other causes of slenderness, from chemotherapy to thyroid dysfunction to heroin addiction to simple genetic luck. Numerous studies have shown that people ascribe any number of negative characteristics to those they consider overweight—they presume they are lazy, gluttonous, unhealthy, lack self-control. Fatphobia is the last socially acceptable form of discrimination—no one gets cancelled for making fat jokes. Hefty humans are less likely to get a date or obtain employment, and when they do get a job, they may be paid less than thinner peers doing the same work. They are less likely to receive accurate medical diagnoses and appropriate treatments. It is considered acceptable for anyone from doctors to family to strangers on the street to comment on their body, admonish them to change it. It is understood they will have more value as a person if they comply.

I haven't cried in years, not at the last two funerals I attended, not when I packed boxes and loaded them in the truck as my husband of 18 years moved out, not when I had to tell our child that his family's form had forever changed. Yet beholding the corpulent man as he lets the water embrace him, knowing the mountain of shame society heaps on him, I feel an unfamiliar welling behind my eyes. I do not yield to the tears, but it startles me to know they still exist, that this stranger could summon them.

I had no such sympathy for myself as I was berated in the locker room while changing from workout gear into swimwear. I couldn't hide from the woman hissing, "You fat cow. How can you bear to be seen like that? Don't you know what everyone thinks of you? You should hide in a hole." She followed me from my locker to the bathroom to the shower to the poolroom, hurling criticisms.

I couldn't escape her because she was me.

I just re-started my gym membership after fourteen months of avoiding public places. Now fully vaccinated, I finally feel comfortable returning to a space with shared air. But my body tells the story of staying home during lockdowns. Of living in a city that erupted into violence after the death of George Floyd on its streets: murders at a 25-year high, assaults rampant, long nighttime walks no longer a safe option for a lone woman.

I never noticed before that there are mirrors everywhere here. Over the sinks, across from the showers, above a long counter with stools in front of it, on the end of every row of lockers. Why is everyone obsessed with looking at themselves before and after working out? I do not even own a full-length mirror—I left ours behind when we moved years ago, hoping to quiet the commentary that started up every time I caught sight of myself. The locker room's unflattering fluorescent lights illuminate my pasty skin, wan after the long Minnesota winter. Everywhere I turn, there is a reminder that my one-piece and swim shorts stretch tighter than before across my plus-size form. I am mortified by how poorly they fit, by the back rolls they expose. By what I have become.

I know I should be grateful to have a body that survived the pandemic when so many did not. As a feminist, I could lecture on the multibillion-dollar beauty and weight loss industries, how they create our insecurities and then monetize our suffering for profit. I know logically that my worth is not determined by the circumference of my waist. But these facts wobble against the weight of other words. My mother's constant stream of criticism played on repeat from earliest memory. The way my body has been referred to by other family members, husband, friends, lovers, medical professionals, random strangers in public places. What I know to be true and how I feel are completely dissociated from each other.

I gaze at the massive man with whorls of water swirling around his torso, the same water roiling against my aching muscles. We are in this pool together, in this world together. I do not see a glutton, a failure, a freak. I do not see my first abuser, the woman whose excess of flesh drives my hatred of my own. I do not see a person whose attractiveness it is my job to judge. I simply see the light in him.

Maybe this practice will help me see the same light in myself.

Hunger

Whitney Vale

The ghost of a starved girl haunts the refrigerator. Her transparent body glimpsed behind the expired tub of Greek plain yogurt. She shivers in the freezer clasping the sorbet. Tiny fingers tap against saltines in the cupboard.

Fifty years ago, I could have rattled off the calories of anything forked, spooned, sipped, or picked. I am still haunted by diet culture, body dysmorphia and Zoom. It shocks me to realize I have half a century of dis-affection for my body. During my extreme diet all those years ago, the scale hovered around 100 pounds, and once, to my delight, 99.

The phrase "anorexia nervosa" had entered mainstream awareness by the early 70's. But it had been used in medical circles for over 100 years. The act of self-starvation had been a spiritual practice in medieval times. There is a timeline for this "wasting disease" and its various names and manifestations on *Eatingrecovery.com.*

My own experience with self-starvation started when I was a theatre major in college. I had dreams of becoming a working actress. To that end I became a professional apprentice at my regional theatre company, while still carrying the minimum hours required to be considered a full-time student. I had gained weight in my last few years of high school. By the time I entered my freshman year of college I was, oh—what are the words—buxom, Rubenesque, pleasingly plump (my father's choice phrase, which I hated). Pleasingly plump could refer to a pigeon or a stuffed turkey.

The Artistic Director of the regional theatre company had a little flirtatious chat with me. He suggested that if I wanted to be more versatile, if I wanted more lead roles, I would need to lose some weight. I felt myself blush. I had not realized my body had been observed and had been found lacking in castability—unless as a character, a side role, a foil perhaps. I felt unattractive. It felt so odd to know he flirted as he leaned across a theatre seat and spoke in a conspiratorial whisper. The signals mixed with judgement. He might as well have used the phrase "pleasingly plump."

I decided to go on one of the most popular diets of the time: Stillman's high protein, low carb diet. I ate bananas and skim milk every day and drank buckets of water. I stayed on it for months and lost a huge amount of weight, the exact pounds I no longer remember. But I went down from a size 16 to a size 6. Weren't the delicate shadows of my rib cage a sign of beauty? I built a false mirror that even now I must smash daily.

For almost a year, not understanding what a maintenance diet meant, I simply underate, keeping my caloric intake well under 1,500.

Then someone showed me some photographs taken from a theatre party. I flipped through and stopped at one image of a female figure who looked like a concentration camp survivor. Something in me lurched, a twist in my shriveled gut. I realized, to my horror, that person was me. I knew I had to eat, but I had no appetite. I tried to remember what foods gave me any pleasure. And I thought of one. Ice cream. Ice cream rescued me. I began to eat ice cream for dinner. My taste buds came alive.

§

Over the course of my life, I have gained and lost weight, but I never experienced the extreme weight loss of my 19th year. I understood that girl layer by layer as I sought help through available literature and support groups. I understood I had been a good girl and people pleaser. I understood that I had not felt any independence—I couldn't even drive—and that the only thing I could control was the carrot stick, the broccoli floret, the half cup of cottage cheese. A dish of banana slices.

Now, I allow indulgence. And I rarely get on a scale unless it is at a doctor's office. Each digit can still feel like a small pinch that I must breathe into and allow. I have other concerns now. My aging body, my post-menopausal body and post-cancer body, my rounded belly and thinning hair. I sigh with relief to hear Jamie Lee Curtis's declaration to be "pro-aging." I look to actresses, mostly British, who have disdained plastic surgery as models of healthy self-image. After vainly struggling with Body Positivity, which always sounds like Bossy Positivity, I am now working slowly toward Body Neutrality. I am slamming the pantry door to scatter the ghosts of diets past.

I look in the mirror, admire my posture, lean in for a conspiratorial whisper, "looking good, sweetheart." As I smile, my dimples deepen, the dimples of the girl I was and the girl beneath my skin. What do I say to you now, ghost-girl? You are lovable just as you are. Don't reduce yourself for anyone.

The Count

Andrew Baise

It's all a numbers game. A stochastic calculation based on biological processes. Did I drink too little water? Did I overeat that night before? What number will my scale spit out and will it ruin my day? The way I obsess over the blinking red jackpot on the digital display of my scale puts accountants, golfers, and loan sharks to shame.

After the day's lucky numbers, a different game unfolds, starting with the very first thing I put in my mouth. "There are approximately 300 calories in this bagel and if I eat a salad for lunch, I will only be at 600 calories for the day, which means I get to have a snack and because I am doing so well, I can have some crackers and cheese instead of the banana I packed with my lunch, which was an emergency provision in case I got greedy and ate the Taco del Mar that was being catered to the office. And even though I ate only a small southwestern salad, I can't eat one of the cookies I smuggled home from lunch, swaddled in a cheap coarse paper towel, for an after-dinner snack. Actually, I can if I work out, which will put me at 1800 calories exactly, assuming I use the elliptical for 20 minutes, which burns approximately 270 calories according to the heart rate monitor on the machine. I should also lift weights while I am at the gym and work out my legs because I don't want to look disproportional from all the climbing I am doing, and of course, I have to do core as well because I will never truly be attractive to anyone until I have a flat stomach. Well, not flat actually, but chiseled. That will never happen, though, because I ended up eating that contraband cookie after dinner, and even though I did three sets of ten reps with three different exercises for three different muscles groups (that is 270 individual reps for anyone keeping count), I still am going to lie awake at night dreading the readout on the scale the next morning which will tell me that the cookie has increased my weight by 0.2 pounds and that I am ugly and undisciplined."

And all of this is, of course, healthy. It is healthy to count calories. It keeps me in good shape and what is good for my body must be good for my mind. The two are connected after all. I know without a crumb of a doubt, that health is wealth, and right now, I am cashing in harder than any loan shark could possibly imagine.

Belly

Nina B. Lichtenstein

In the days and weeks after the birth of each of my three sons, I looked down on my belly and found it alien. My tummy was mushy and (still!) big and made me wonder if it could possibly contain another munchkin? Nobody told me about *that* part of the childbearing process—the post-partum lumpy bleeding, the lingering cramps, the unfamiliar shape of my body, despite the baby being out. I was lucky to be able to nurse all three boys, as this turns out to be nature's way to expedite the maternal body's return to "normalcy." Except, of course, there is no "return," just a new normal, which I have found is one of the hardest but also most valuable lessons that applies to most things in life.

As life happens, it takes its toll on a belly, not just from childbearing, as probably most middle-aged women *sans enfants* can attest to; we're in this never-ending morphing business together. My waistline, hips and belly kept expanding each year, and although I've always been physically active, my weight hit an all-time high at the same time my husband Brian hit his midlife crisis.

§

My father was recovering from lung cancer surgery in 2005, just as I turned forty and was about to finish my PhD. The convergence of these three events felt momentous, an urgent call to action: my dad's life so imminently threatened, and mine, so definitely mid-way, combined with the completion (finally!) of my doctorate after many years of postponing the last hurdle— the dissertation—due to childrearing; I had earned an adventure, dammit.

"Pappa, I have an idea," I said on the phone, relieved Dad had pulled through the surgery okay and didn't need chemo or radiation. "How about I come home to Norway with the boys for a year, so we can spend some quality time together?" I hoped the prospect of having us near would boost his spirits and help him heal.

"Really? Oh honey, that would be something special," he said. I could hear it on his breath that he got emotional.

I don't remember what came first, me mentioning to Brian I wanted to take a year in Norway or me making a promise to my dad. I do know I was not going to be dissuaded; this was one of those existential moments when you just know it's the thing you must do to live with yourself and not have regrets.

Brian agreed reluctantly, ceding to my wishes because he knew how much my dad meant to me and how important it was for our boys to get to know him better. Brian and I always said we'd go live in Norway for a while, so our kids could become comfortable in my culture and language (after all, I had converted to Judaism and immigrated to the U.S. to make a life with him), but his business made it impossible for him to plan any long-term absence. He was supposed to "commute" to come see me and the kids in Oslo every six weeks, but he never traveled easily, and the logistics of remote work (pre-Covid era) made it difficult, which resulted in months going by without us being together as a family.

Meanwhile, alone at home in Connecticut, he used his newfound free time to turn himself into a chiseled Adonis practicing and teaching Brazilian jiu jitsu, his passion. To his evolving new look, he added a "soul patch" (the small patch of facial hair just below the lower lip) and wore Under Armor black spandex skullcaps over his shaved, bald head. With his 6'4" 260lbs frame, he made for an impressive presence.

About mid-year, I was waiting for him with butterflies in my stomach at the Oslo airport arrivals, enjoying the sight of loved ones reuniting. I always loved when we'd meet at the airport after a separation, a new and exciting discovery yet a grounding reunion with familiar smells and touches. But when Brian finally walked through the electronic doors, I could tell something was off right away.

"Look at you!" I said in surprise, measuring him up and down. I couldn't make myself compliment his svelte appearance in his soul-patched macho state. Something hit me in the gut as a turn-off. It was as if we were two same poles of magnets that, when put together, repel each other.

Despite my visceral reaction at the airport, we had a sweet homecoming at our apartment as the boys returned from school and found their pappa on the couch with a great big smile and open arms. After the kids went to bed, he ran his big, strong hands over my hips and belly, a touch I typically loved.

"Why didn't you get rid of this excess?" he asked, measuring my curves with his eyes and grip. "Didn't you say that life in Norway would be super healthy, and that you'd get into shape?"

I mumbled something about not having time to work out since single parenting and a new, full-time job as a high school teacher was overwhelming.

"These love-handles aren't exactly a turn on, you know," he continued. A wave of defensiveness came over me and disgust for how he carried himself. A clown, I thought, fuming. I took my pillow and blanket and slept, wounded, on the couch that night.

§

The next time my belly is flat as a pancake and love handles gone, we are separated and in the throes of divorce. I'm "skinny" and get lots of compliments both from Brian and my surroundings about how great I look, but of course, I feel like shit. I wake up with stomach aches in the morning and go to bed numbed from too much wine or bourbon or both. I get through the day with the help of Zoloft and Xanax. I add Ambien to the mix at night to ensure at least six hours of oblivious rest. I had become a beautifully skinny, miserable, forty-five-year-old woman.

It was during this wretched period that, for the only time in my life, I forgot to eat regular meals and lost so much weight that I fit into my size 8 wedding gown for the first time since 1988, when I was twenty-three. I recall how awesome *and* how awful it felt when the zipper of the Laura Ashley brocade dress closed with ease, and I decided to wear it to my synagogue's Purim carnival, a cardboard sign around my neck reading "Mail Order Bride."

"Wow, you look fabulous!" people exclaimed.

While the world around me offered enthusiasm and positive feedback about my appearance, I was never more broken. The drugs sailed me through the emotional fog with a chemically induced glow.

§

Ten years later, as I'm watching *The Crown* on Netflix, my hand runs over the softness of my middle-aged belly, bloated after my partner Tony and I had just enjoyed a dinner of veggie burgers with Swiss cheese and oven baked sweet potato fries. I sip an Allagash White straight from the bottle, while Tony pours his into a stemmed glass, letting the foaming head reach past the top of the glass, just the way he likes it. I'm slumped comfortably on the couch next to him, as Queen Elizabeth's coronation is about to take place with much pomp and circumstance. My belly is covered by the light cotton of my long and shapeless summer dress. I am happy.

§

My hips and stomach are the two areas of my body over which I feel the least control; these are the body parts that have morphed into their own independent nations during the throes of menopause, as if a riotous and expansionist tyrant is at the helm. Where will it all end?

Perhaps it's time to act. But that will require the full cooperation of all parts of the body-nation, especially the control tower up top, which of late has proven to be disturbingly (or is it liberatingly?) laissez-faire, in favor of a gluttonous enjoyment of life's consumable pleasures. *What the heck is this all about?* I'm tempted to ask. But I already know: women my age often arrive at a point in our lives when we decide it's not worth the battle anymore. Let bellies be soft and bulbous, hips wide and grabbable, underarms wobbly; life is too short to struggle where no struggle is needed.

When It Hurts

There is Not Only One Kind of Pain

Jennifer Fliss

Deep in the Catskills, under the watchful eyes of twin rounded mountain tops, I have a headache. It is in the gloaming after a dinner of chicken nuggets and purple bug juice and before the evening activity, which might be a talent show, a scavenger hunt, or an inter-camp hockey game. I trek up the small hill to the cabin with the word "infirmary" etched in its wood. Children line up on benches in a room that smells of Pledge and Band-Aids. The children are stuck together where their sweaty arms touch. Ailments. Allergy shots. Attention-seekers. Thermometers shoved in mouths. Little cups of grape liquid swallowed. Bandages slapped on.

I have a headache, I say to the purple light. Purple white. A throbbing gel in front of my eyes. It's distinct from the evening sunlight outside, where we just raised the flag. Or was that this morning? In the dewy morning in a circle around the flagpole, we sat in lines by bunk. Announcements. Color war is coming. Visiting Day is coming. Camp Lokanda is coming for the sophomores' soccer tournament. I suck at soccer. Asthma. Terrible runner. Hard breathing, kicked in the shins and in the ribs and shoved to the ground by girls wearing woven friendship bracelets. I stay down, embedded in the wet morning grass, loamy, cool, and I almost mistake it for a friend.

Food waiter, waiter, waiter. Food waiter, waiter. My bunkmates chant in the dining room for sub-par food and juice. My head pounds, but still I sing along too. We bang our hands on the table. The next table joins in. Then the next. Soon the whole dining hall is at it. Feral wolves demanding their grub. I feel the pack of them in this one spot above my right temple. In fact, there's a hand dance for this obnoxious chant. Pound table in this order:

Fist

Thumb

Pointer & middle fingers

Pointer & pinky finger.

Begin again and chant: *Food waiter, waiter, waiter. Food waiter, waiter.* Try both hands at the same time.

It is a wonder we aren't slapped when we return home at the end of our two-month stint at sleepaway camp. Were we heathens when we arrived or did we become these animals away from the grasp of our parents?

I have a headache, I say to the camp nurse. A thermometer is jabbed into my mouth. *No fever,* the nurse says, but leaves the glass stick in my mouth. My head hurts. No fever. You're fine. I try to worry the mercury with my tongue, please let my temperature rise. I don't want to go back to my bunk. For many reasons, really. But the physical pain right now is more than the other kinds of pain. All of a sudden, I vomit. The thermometer is thrust to the ground. *Thought you had a headache,* the nurse scoffs. *I don't know. I'm eight.* I say or maybe I don't say, but just think. Sour and cruel in my mouth. I want for water, but I wait until they can come to their conclusion before I ask. They don't offer.

They don't understand migraines back then. I don't either. But I intimately know the fluorescence of lights and the mallets beating in my head. I know the welling in my esophagus, the brine of vomit, the queasy quaking sleep-won't-come pain.

The vomit stops them, these nurses who are just mothers of other campers. Orange, yellow, brownish – the chicken nuggets from dinner. I'm assigned a bunk bed in infirmary room three. No one shares the room, but the next day, sickies are watching *Blade Runner* in room two. I am lightheaded from the day-before pain; the hangover of the innocent. I linger at the doorjamb watching the probably-inappropriate-for-our-age film and feel like I'm hallucinating, coming into the middle of the film like that. The movie's labyrinthine setting will stay with me for decades and I think of it every time a migraine comes on.

Visiting Day is in a week and I already know what it will look like. The night before pink razors will be wielded by nine-year-olds to shave their prepubescent legs and warn the child that isn't yet ready. Then, on a mountain bright day, Mercedes and limos will climb the hill into camp. Moms and their manicures. Dads and their golf tans. Our Civic hatchback trundles up the hill under my father's weight and the weight of domestic tragedy. I don't run to my parents as my bunkmates do. I wait until, at last, they arrive at my bunk. He, heaving with his heft and the walk of a great distance. She, tired from her lifelong limp. Both with nothing in their arms for me. Both, saying little, aside from asking me if I had spoken to any adults about anything that goes on in our house. Apparently people have been asking around. *No, I've said nothing. Good, now show us your bunk.*

At this point, my hope is that all the other campers will take off with their dearly missed parents. They'll leave camp for Woodstock or show them the latest waterskiing skill they mastered. They do this, but not before a snide remark about the way my mother walks or to point out the weird kid to their coiffed parents. I try to bow out of family activities with the excuse of a headache. It isn't always untrue.

Often, parents bring "bunk gifts." A gift for each child in the bunk. Pulled aside, I am told, that there isn't enough for everyone. Ten in the bunk. *My mom only brought nine,* they said to me in the back closet room. I won't receive a t-shirt with Bugs Bunny coming out of the chest pocket. I say, *oh sure, no big deal,* assure them that it's okay, my butterfly heart reverting to its cocoon. The next night: *hey, why don't we all wear our new matching shirts!?*

My migraines are real, torrential, appalling. But also, a respite when needed. I bow out of canteen, of the attempt to look like I have friends. Instead I find something fascinating in the grass or within the old color war banners hung on the walls of the Rec Hall. *Caribbean Green! Aussie White!* We won color war that year–1988, my first year as a camper. I'd been getting headaches for at least two years already. I use my headaches to retire to the bunk early, pretend I'm asleep when they all come in shrieking and laughing an hour later.

Still I return for years and years and eventually become a counselor. The girls are different. The Umbro shorts and the neon track suits are gone. They don't wear string friendship bracelets anymore either. Now they're Tiffany charm bracelets with silver hearts with their initials on them. They wear them all day. For soccer, tennis, horseback riding. They go nowhere without their precious dog tags. Gifts from daddy.

The girls are the same. I see a small camper pushed into gravel. I hear jokes about weight, about hair, about being dirty. The "it" girls still iron their curls nightly before canteen, where they play ping pong and get Charleston Chews which will get stuck in their braces. No one here makes fun of kids with braces. Money gets you orthodontia. These children come from Short Hills and Dix Hills and all kinds of hills that people like me trudge up with giant boulders. No wonder my head hurts all the time.

At the infirmary, at eight, I milk my pain for all it's worth. After the pounding stops. After I sleep. After the hangover has ebbed. After I have more energy for reading and imaginings. I imagine people care. Envision my counselors coming to check on me. *Are you feeling better? We missed you!* None of that happens and on a soggy morning, the vapor of dew low on the ground, I clutch my pajamas and head back to my bunk. There, under the beguiling whispers of Cat Stevens, my bunkmates are sweeping and making their beds. Something they never do at home. My bedsheets are flung all around. It had been made when I left for the infirmary the day before. When I pull back my blanket, I find mounds of shaving cream in sherbet colors. I can feel their eyes on my back as I discover their treason.

Later, these children will become doctors and lawyers, schoolteachers warning their students about bullying. Their children will return to the same camp. Migraines will become moderately more understood as a chronic illness. I will write my imaginings down, a pretend world that I've turned into a career. This summer, I will be sending my daughter to camp. Not that camp. But still. She doesn't get migraines. Mine continue. Reminders of when my heart pounded too hard for its container.

Body Out of Water

Suzanne Hicks

The time I walked into the Caribbean Sea, rocky earth under my feet and I outstretched my arms for balance as my body swayed with the current. I held onto your hand, newly married to mine.

The time I watched you in the Pacific Ocean hopping over waves. My legs unsteady, I stayed behind on the lounge chair. You emerged smiling, buzzing back to me with exhilaration fresh on your face, a simple pleasure I was certain I'd never experience again.

The time we stayed on Coronado Island and you pushed me out to the ocean in the beach wheelchair that we rented. I pressed my toes into the sand and water washed over them. I watched you wander in, briefly, only up to your knees, and I was thankful the water was cold.

The time I watched from my chair as you went down stairs leading to the expansive shore in Mexico. You took a photo for another couple on the beach and jealous tears stung my eyes as I witnessed them create a memory that we could not.

The time I first used a lift to lower myself into chlorinated water where I anxiously grabbed the pool noodle, you helping me saddle it between my legs so I could stay afloat. Because all the drugs infused into my veins, injected under my skin, in pills that I swallowed, along with countless visits to physical therapy, handfuls of supplements and special diets couldn't stop me from arriving at that moment.

Pain's Imposter Syndrome

Barb Mayes Boustead

"*Faker.*"

They whispered it in my middle school classes when I left three minutes early to avoid the crush of clumsy bodies between class periods.

They rolled their eyes on the sidelines when I sat out gym class, again. The gym teacher joined them.

They taunted me with it on the playground, running around me in circles when I could not escape.

Until somebody experiences disability, they have no idea how painful it is to be the one who is different, walking with assistive devices or on crutches yet again. Middle schoolers prey like feral dogs on weaker members of their own pack.

"You keep switching legs."

Before doctors knew to treat it with physical therapy and supportive treatments, severe Osgood-Schlatter Disease was debilitating, treated with immobilization and rest. It also was something I could point to on an X-ray and document. See? There it is. That's the bone that's in the wrong place and the squeeze it's putting on the knee joint space. I had it in both legs, presenting pain in both of them intermittently.

When the Osgood-Schlatter X-ray presentation faded but the pain continued, it was harder to understand. An orthopedic surgeon who treated athletes at Michigan State scoped the knee to find and fix what was wrong, but outside of an irritated joint lining and a few tiny bone chips, he could find no structural trigger for the pain and swelling.

"Hey, gimp. Do I get to leave early with you if I carry your books?"

Physical therapy, slower growth, and a little luck helped the pain and swelling ease after three years of being on crutches or in full-leg braces more often than not. The pain and swelling would return intermittently, though—a suddenly swollen knee after a busy set of shifts at work, the other knee activating a year or two later after humping boxes into a new house, then back to the first after climbing a ladder a few too many times. Another orthopedic surgeon, another round of physical therapy, another scope, another diagnosis of "synovitis" and "inflammation," code words for "the ligaments and cartilage are fine, but the knee is swelling without a known cause."

By my 20s, even I started to question if I was faking it. Why did the pain show up with no cause? Why did the joint swell, and despite ice and anti-inflammatory medications and physical therapy and cortisone injections, refuse to depart until the joint was breached and drained and checked by someone with an M.D.?

It's because everybody has pain, I decided. I was no special snowflake; I was just seeking attention from doctors for my pain and swelling when other people clearly were suffering in silence. Surely others felt pain far worse than mine.

The middle-school voices invaded my head, merging with my worst thoughts and becoming my own.

Just power through it. Suck it up, buttercup. Live with it, like everybody else does.

My mantra became, "If it isn't actually damaged, it isn't worth going to the doctor." Pain isn't damage. Pain doesn't deserve attention.

Swelling was another story. It signaled that something might actually be damaged, and it needed a doctor's needle to drain it away. In a bargain with myself, I determined that just one aching and swollen joint wasn't enough. Two at once, though, sent me in. Buy one, get one free.

An attentive orthopedic surgeon took notice of a knee and a toe both swollen, inflamed, and aching. His tests on the fluid extracted by needle from the knee confirmed his suspicion: systemic, chronic inflammatory arthritis. The pain and swelling had a cause, a label, a measurable marker in the fluid's white blood cell count. It wasn't all in my mind. He passed me on to a rheumatologist, one of those champions of indeterminate pain.

Clad in a back-tying cloth gown and chilly at my initial diagnostic appointment with a rheumatologist, I waited to be judged. The old doctor, slow and careful, examined me from head to toe and took inventory of everything that hurt with handwritten notes on a clipboard fat with papers.

His questions confused me. Did he want me to talk about every ache, or just today's aches? How far back? Just the bad ones, or every pesky twinge?

"All of it," he said. "Everything."

I followed him top to bottom, backtracking as I recalled that indeed, this shoulder or that hip had given me pain that I'd compartmentalized and buried until now. I talked about pains I'd never said out loud. I'd never had a doctor ask so many questions or take so long to talk to me.

"I had no idea you had so much pain all the time," my partner, Josh, said in awe when the doctor stepped out. He had accompanied me to the appointment for moral support. Though we had known each other for years, I'd kept the inventory of my pain since childhood mostly to myself, except when it snuck out for those knee scopes.

"Everyone has some pains all the time," I shrugged with absolute sincerity.

"No," he said gently. "They don't."

"I mean, you don't," I said, "but most people do."

"No," he repeated. "They really don't."

He fixed his kind, wide-open hazel eyes on me. I blinked and squirmed on the noisy exam-room table paper, trying to process what he said. It took days, maybe even longer. In privacy later, I sobbed.

If everyone didn't have pain all the time, then my internal dialog had been lying to me. The protective layers of gaslighting in my mind broke down, leaving me without a buffer from the sharp cruelty of those middle school years. I wasn't being a baby or a faker. I had been a child, in pain, lacking empathy from peers and some adults. I had been bullied into accepting pain as normal. I'd wasted more than a decade enduring pain in silence.

And still, the path to diagnosis with autoimmune conditions is bumpy and winding and twisted. The symptoms almost fit this condition or that, but not quite. Blood tests rule out some diseases, but almost no autoimmune conditions have confident yes-or-no tests. Their diagnosis relies on symptom analysis, trust in doctors, trust in self-assessment, and the process of elimination.

Lupus.

Not BAD lupus, though. Marginal lupus. Minor lupus. Low-grade lupus. Inconvenient lupus.

Even still, after the epiphany that constant pain is not a universal human experience, doubt lingers about the worthiness of the disease in my body, of my experience with it, of the way I handle it.

Even still, questions about how much pain I'm in confuse me. How can I put my pain on a scale of 1 to 10? I've never known zero, and I'm certain I haven't yet felt the worst pain a human can experience, which is what a 10 should be. Isn't it always in the middle? Am I supposed to rate the hum of the constant pain or the intermittent sharp peaks? Does that annoying neck pain count when I know it's just a tight muscle? If that pain felt like a 6 on its first day and hasn't changed in the week I've learned to live with it, is it still a 6 or has it downgraded to a 4? Pain no more belongs on a finite number scale than love.

Every year, I learn more about what autoimmune disease means in my body. I deserve to at least try to find treatments that will make me feel less pain, swelling, and fatigue. All the symptoms of my body matter. Telling my partner about them invites him to be a part of the solution and to support my voice when it wavers. Telling doctors about them is advocating for my health. My symptoms deserve medical attention and treatment. And I will grow into admitting, someday, that my (MY) lupus is a (MY) disability.

I couldn't bully away my pain any more than the bullies around me could; now, I choose to let it speak. Honoring the voice of my pain includes paying attention to it, relaying it to my medical team, and avoiding comparing it with the pain of others. We're still learning to trust each other—me, to trust that my pain is telling the truth, and my body, to trust that I will take the information it gives me to seek relief and assistance and comfort.

Untangling from years of doubt, the voices in my head are learning new language.

I hear you. Take a break. Take the medication. Rest. You are safe.

Men and Their Hands

Claudia Monpere

Their goddamn hands.

§

Is there a formula for how much loving touch it takes from a good man to erase angry touches from that other man? That husband man? This good man touches me only with affection or desire but there was that one time he nudged me—gently—to move faster because my slow walking was blocking a car trying to back up and I lost it and screamed at him to get his goddamn hands off me.

§

Touch is the first sense to develop in utero and the last sense, along with hearing, to vanish when we're dying.

§

You could call it dying, the sex life between my husband and me. Penetration was terribly painful, and my male OB-GYN said only that everything looked normal. My husband loved my body. He wished my hair wasn't so short. But he had high praise for everything else. None of that mattered. Everything I did in bed made him anxious or mad. Especially when I tried too hard, like asking him how he wanted to be touched. That was something I should know.

§

Anyone in an abusive relationship knows the job description is hefty. It includes mind reading.

§

One would think I was an inexperienced lover. It was my husband who was a virgin. I'd had four lovers before him. All was fine with them. I didn't think much about my body during my twenty-four-year marriage. No shame but certainly no pride. In my life, I've rarely spent more than a few minutes in front of a mirror except as an adolescent obsessed with my complexion and so disgusted by my curly hair that I had my mother iron it. I guess my body was a workhorse for having my babies, commuting to work, driving the kids to school and soccer practice, doing physical therapy for back pain, scrubbing cat vomit out of the carpet.

No, wait, my body was a place for tenderness. Crouched at pond's edge as my hands touched my children's tiny fingers helping them wrap bologna on a long stick and fish for crawdads, then gently returning them to the water; rolling on grass, our bodies smooshed together; wiping s'more sticky fingers and snuggling in front of campfires. My toes for This Little Piggy. Fingers for The Eensy Weensy Spider. My belly button for ding-dong.

§

My husband and I separated when the kids were seven and twelve. His idea. His girlfriend's young lovely body and bouncy blonde hair. My weight gain and dead-end dates: the man who stared at my breasts throughout dinner, the man who droned on about his folklore research, the man who told me about every diet he'd been on, lifting his shirt to show all the flab left after his huge weight loss.

§

I said no when my husband wanted to move back home. We were nearly finished with the divorce paperwork. My body had begun to relax, the back pain mostly gone, the facial numbness the neurologist never figured out but that occurred sometimes when I was around my husband— that numbness vanished.

Then the doorbell rang. 6:14 am on a Monday morning. The policeman reported my husband's car—keys and wallet inside—abandoned on the San Francisco Bay Bridge. I abandoned my body. Sure, it was there to comfort my children, there for family and friends' loving hugs. It was there for police and coastguard, teachers and therapists and lawyers and insurance adjustors with their endless forms. It machined its way through days but the me part of it that connected to people, that could feel emotions, that rarely forgot anything, that reveled in daily sensory details, the me of my body was gone. Every tree, person, or building I looked at was one dimensional. Sounds seemed too close or too far away. The taste of everything was gray.

§

The years, oh, the years. The children and I bumbled our way through grief. We grew older. I watched my body age through several long, loving but impermanent relationships. I spent more time in front of a mirror—counting wrinkles, watching my jawline begin to sag. But my hair; something happened to my hair. Always a curly, quiet mess, so uncontrollable I kept it very short, it was silent no more. Take care of me, it demanded. Let me make my curls. I found a hair stylist who knew some things about curly hair. I grew my hair and reveled in the soft curls that had been dormant. There was actually a part of my body I was proud of.

And sex, oh sex. Now I can call it making love and not feel like I'm lying. I never understood the intimacy of loving sex. But now with this good man who is my life partner, I get it. Oh, do I get it. The pain during sex with my husband? Never with this man. When I was younger, I dismissed the mind/body connection. But damn if my vagina wasn't having her say. Who wants to share their body with someone whose mouth fissures rage? But who writes love poems to you if he's having that kind of day?

I want to write love poems to me, to my body. I want to cherish it in spite of a hearing loss and graying hair and arthritis, grateful for all it can do as it ferries me through the years. I used to take comfort in the fact I would be dead someday. Now I take comfort in the fact that I have this dazzling day. May it multiply for decades.

How We Show Up in the World—
And How the World Sees Us

My Body Is a Language That I Cannot Speak

Claude Olson

1. I have begun to suspect that this world is not my own. Or perhaps, more accurately, this body I possess is somehow otherworldly. It is a spectacle unto itself, able to draw an audience without a promise of performance. Passing strangers stare as it walks by. Some take photos to prove what they have seen. I suddenly find myself on display before a crowd of gawking anthropologists. No one tells them to stop tapping on the glass.

2. And yet there is no other world I can claim to be from. I was born in American suburbia, raised among humans who look nothing like me. To them, I have a genetic mutation, a typo in my DNA, a body in an alternate spelling. This renders me disabled by one-sided comparison. My arms and legs are disproportionate to my torso. My height is far below average. But what if *they* are the disproportionate ones, towering two feet over my head? What if everyone who thinks I am a dwarf is really a giant? What if I wasn't always the oddity?

3. A young boy sits next to me on the Metro. He cannot be older than seven but no one seems to be watching him. The child is perplexed by me, by the fact that we are the same height yet I am clearly an adult. He glances down at my legs, noticing how they bow like a pair of crescent moons. *What happened to you?* he asks. I am not sure how to respond. I, too, am searching for the answer.

4. How can I explain life inside a paradox? I have achondroplasia, a rare condition that can be found in every corner of the world. There are people with bodies like mine across every ethnicity, country, and social class. We all share a mutant gene yet we are not related by blood. If not for that one bit of DNA, we would look like a random sample of the

human race. There is no family tree to connect us, no shared point of origin. Each of us is an ordinary alien. Together, we are without a home planet.

5. What is it like to live in a world where every body is like your own? Any world filled with bodies like mine is an entirely fictional realm. Think about the Munchkins, the Oompa Loompas, and the Seven Dwarves. Imagine watching a film, seeing a country full of caricatures, people with bright green hair, garish make-up, bodies that are comical because they are too ridiculous to exist. Now imagine your body looks more like those than almost any in the real world. Would you begin to wonder if you, too, are fantastical?

6. I must remind myself that, somehow, we are everywhere. There are 30,000 little people in the United States and 650,000 across the globe. But those are merely numbers. All I can prove is that there are two: me and my mother.

7. I imagine her as an ignorant child, sitting inches away from the television set, transfixed by *The Wizard of Oz*. As Dorothy wakes up in a technicolor world, I picture my mother's eyes growing wide. Did she realize her world would soon change just as drastically? Did a flicker of recognition pass across her face as the Munchkins led Dorothy down the yellow brick road? Then I remember: she grew up with a black-and-white TV, in a town where the roads were not yellow, only varying shades of gray.

8. Before me, my mother was the only little person on the family tree. For most of her childhood, she was unaware of this. No one told her that she was any different, that she acquired a spontaneous mutation, or that she wouldn't grow up in the same way most everyone else does. Her body was both a rarity and an open secret. She must have spent her childhood looking up at the ceilings and believing she'd one day touch them. She

must have waited patiently for her growth spurt to hit and noticed that everyone else was growing faster than she could keep up with, that the ceilings continued to be out of reach. She must have woken up one day with a startling revelation: she was unlike anyone she had ever met.

9. I think about how my grandparents hid my mother's disability for a decade and I wonder: Is there something about our bodies we should be ashamed of? Does the truth of our skeletal fate bar us from a happy, peaceful life, or at least a normal one? Or would it be easier if we did not know we were always the exceptionally small elephants in the room?

10. My mother was born an emperor, convinced that she wore beautiful clothes. I was born completely aware of the fact that I was naked.

11. How can I explain being raised inside a paradox? My mother never hid the truth about my body yet she was unknowingly telling a different sort of lie. She believed my body was a perfect replica of her own. *I assumed whatever I'd have, you'd have*, she tells me. We both thought we were a world of two, when really we still floated in our own separate orbits.

12. At sixteen, I discovered that the world found me deformed. My body was its own open secret. My mother was the first to realize that we were no longer mirror images. While she was slim and as straight as a stunted body could be, I was heavy and meandering, curvy because of both my weight and my bones. My mother chose not to tell me what was happening. She found someone else to break the news.

13. That afternoon in the orthopedic surgeon's office comes back to me like a dream: a stranger and my mother in the same room, no one acting as they should. When we arrived, the surgeon asked me to take off my pants. My mother did not object. I begrudgingly stripped down to my faded yellow underwear and walked back and forth for the man I had just met. I stared at the tile floor so I did not have to see him study my naked legs. He wanted an X-ray of them too and asked me to stand

against a wall. It felt like he was taking my mug shot. I wondered what I had done wrong.

14. It was then I realized my mother and I were entirely different creatures. She was a human who just happened to be short. I was an alien who couldn't resemble anything but a freak.

15. In the X-ray, my legs glowed with blue moonlight, bending like a set of parentheses around an empty afterthought. (For a moment, I allowed myself to find them beautiful.) The doctor pointed at my bones with his pen, emphasizing their curvature as if it wasn't already obvious. *There is the option of cosmetic surgery,* he said. This is what I heard: *Under your skin, there is an ugliness that does not belong in this world.* My bones were whole but, just then, I felt entirely broken.

16. What happened to you?

17. Nothing, in the end. We backed out of the surgery when we realized it would not be worth the price, the pain, or the physical therapy. I simply had to live with the fact that I couldn't be fixed.

18. Or maybe, there wasn't anything that I needed to change. I kept walking, in my lilting way, slowly realizing that I am no more strange than my onlookers. *What if I am not the oddity?*

19. Perhaps our beauty is the open secret. People see our alien forms and believe they have made a rare discovery. Once, a man approached my mother at a bar: *Has anyone ever told you that you're beautiful?* She laughs when she tells me this story: my mother is well aware that she is a glorious, technicolor spectacle.

20. Since leaving suburbia, I have discovered my own body's beauty for myself. I moved to Washington and left behind the need to conform. Now, I am a creature in a vibrant city. Strangers often come up to me,

stare deeply into my eyes, and tell me that I am beautiful. I know that they mean this as a revelation but I still take it as a compliment. I have shown them another world—no, an entire universe of possibility.

It's Ableist to Ask Me What I Eat

Camille U. Adams

There's a man I no longer talk to. A grad school peer. A cohort inclusion, a writing partner who thought it fair to repeatedly probe my pancreas, my fridge. My lunch bag, my diet, the ridge developing between my eyebrows when I am asked to figure out how

to say:

my enzymes don't come out to play. Not in the face of bloating wheat and skin erupting grain.

to say:

dairy sends me back to hard white cotton sheets, my feverish engorged body splayed. Sends me back to bitter antibiotics, to venal drips, to nurses injecting alternating butt cheeks, and dark weeklong stays.

Like the six years of my teenage scares in-and-out warded at the General Hospital in Port of Spain. The unknown, speeding ambulance tears through Trinidad streets. Those weeping years before my milk allergy was diagnosed homoeopathically at eighteen. The years I was bedded and bound under those prayed-over, bleach-stink sheets. The years during which my church aunts said their god was cursing miniskirt-wearing me. Cursing my swollen ankles, my swollen feet.

This man poking at the tender centre my shoulders are curling in over. Tightly. When he rudely and repetitively asks me to explain:

how do I even easily Tinder, lemme-take-you-out-for-dinner date if

I have to state that I must cook my every meal. And ensure no soy, no lectins are concealed. No varicose inducing, circulation reducing gelatin among the ingredients. And what I'm not really hungry actually meant is that I spent hours on the internet and in grocery lanes googling the origin of chemical names.

Researching like my life depends on ensuring my colon is in the clear. Absolutely zero dextrose, Midwest masked corn stealing in everywhere. And seeming antisocial is really my being in the throes of listening to my un-cellulitis legs declare, not here!

And this man and me en no donkey years friend fuh him to try and shove and delve. And puncture my silence in badgering violence, Why you don't eat anything that could sit on a shelf? And he fass and out he place to insist and interrogate. To thrust past the perimeter of polite conversation, wresting to pry open unearned vulnerability's gate. To seek to intimate his pushy curiousity requires my satisfying. As if I'm obliged, as if my guarded replying is my lying because I'm not unveiling,

not saying:

my liver does not give a care as to whether I look weird. Liver shrugs if I whine it is not fair I cannot ingest convenient preservatives and hormones and pesticides and HCL fats revered. Sweet restaurants' flair in trendy social media reels widely shared. Not for me, not when Liver must then dispense extra energy to cleanse a toxic flood from my blood that cannot afford to be overwhelmed.

Thus, Kidneys decree:

eat organic only, please. Only live produce. Only veiny, starchy roots strong and sound. Dasheen, cassava, eddo, tania pulled from rested, replenished ground. Only provision that naturally fed. Chambered in biotic, mycelium rich earth into which no chemicals bled.

Eat only of the pure, black soil over which washed, cracked, harvesting hands lovingly toil. Brown hands bathed in the tropical sun. Reaping, sowing all your genetically remembered nutrition. This your body knows. This to keep turgidity out your toes. This. We will have it so.

And that man wasn't even or ever going to be my lover. Unappealing and married to another. So how dare you put my spleen under a microscope, squaring to grope past staved off invasion. This organ filtering your dirty interrogation wanting to uncover:

how my duodenum becomes upset when it doesn't get enough berries and citrus and apples' fibre. And how my ileum well voicey and does conspire to loud up its complaints against cruciferous foods and too much sucrose and too much sodium.

But, for yuh mucousal passages and yuh brain and yuh eyes, bring the Earth Balance soy-free butter come. And smother it nice all over that California Frieda's and A.V. Thomas sweet potato. And all over the steamed spinach, drench it good and slow. Come coat the baked wild caught Alaskan salmon, too. Load up an all the good fats your memory needs to write the truth.

And feed us, this body of yours, charging you a whole mortgage with the clause that your exorbitant Whole Foods and Flatbush Food Co-op bills undeniably will ensure – not the cure – but that we keep at bay the chronic lymphedema your parents did not fight against.

Doh be fraid to say:

no. For your lymphatic system sake. The lymphatic vessels that would not sustain carrying bad-sperm children. That same always saving your life circulatory system. The lymphatic white blood cells that demand you ingest no impurities. The lymphatic fluid that stagnates if dirtied. And causes infections and hospital warding dis-ease.

The lymphatic system that lays you flat. Too wearied to move if it must enact disposal from your supposal you could ever compromise. The lymphatic system that would have you not vie with organisms with which your ancestral body does not comply.

And this man who I no longer talk to signed our budding friendship's demise. On the dotted line when he plunged past my uncomfortable titter, my frown, my voiced reply: I have food allergies, alright.

Signed the goodbye when he kept prodding to inquire. Like the fact that bottled enzymes and probiotics and heeding calls to eat on time being what my gut flora requires is business in which he should be ever mired.

Like my body's mechanisms need his comprehension. Want his witticisms at a duck faeces drenched, toxic land and filthy-stenched, shabby, lakeside café. Which is where we went to write. Where I decline his benevolent offer of a dollar bagel and apparently hurt his chivalrous pride.

The self same gluten heavy bagel he smack and slurp and chew open-mouth and burp to consume. The self same refined carbohydrate bagel he rub he big belly for to make room. The self same processed white flour bagel he peer into my eyes over like he confuse.

This man who I no longer talk to. This man who act like I strange. And refuse in his advanced age to let people's bodies be. To not force, to not plunder a woman's body's privacy.

I felt violated.

So now we do not speak. This man who asked, what *do* you eat? Because I will never pick up my ringing cell for a man by whom my discerning gut is repelled.

The Importance of Shade

Monica Nathan

Mother:

A girl sits at her father's kitchen table, her sari's dupatta draped over her head. She has spent the last twelve years sheltering from the gaze of leering men and the blaze of Kolkata's sun, cultivating an unblemished reputation. Her mother sits to her right, competing with the chaiwala in the alley outside, both promoting their wares.

The word 'wheat-colored' is written on the biodata held loosely in the hands of the older woman sitting opposite. The girl does not dare raise her eyes. She stares instead at the paisley tablecloth until the pattern resembles fish swimming upstream, but she can discern the woman's upright posture from the periphery of her vision. This is their second meeting, and the first time the woman has brought her son.

The girl has memorized his face in two dimensions and her brain works to extrapolate the depth of his lips that now tick off educational achievements and career highlights in a soft baritone. A ceiling fan slices through the air, giving rhythm to his words. She had studied his picture the night before, had placed it on the pillow beside her and pretended to wake up to his bristling moustache. She flushes now, thinking of it.

"What does she cook?" The older woman's voice is authoritative.

"Many delicacies," the girl's mother assures the older woman. "She has been cooking since five years old."

They have already analyzed caste and compared astrological charts. The stars are aligned. It doesn't stop the girl's tumult of emotions, the slight tremor of her fingers.

She is startled to feel the older woman's hand cover her own, but she leans into its warmth, longs to trace the blue veins bulging worm-like in the translucent folds. The older woman rubs her thumb firmly over the girl's wrist, testing to see if her skin is in fact as pale as it seems or camouflage for the trenches.

Daughter:

She lies on a lounger, limbs exposed to the Jamaican sun. Her mother's voice briefly enters her mind. "Eesh, your color will become so dirty." Waves drown out the sound and she focuses instead on the hawkers selling ceramic bowls and beaded jewelry to the tourists dotted along the beach.

Her husband lays sprawled out next to her, droplets of sweat trailing across his salt-stained skin. There is a sudden ballooning in her chest as she takes him in. His already dark complexion has transformed into a burnished copper, and she thinks she might know what beauty is. She is grateful that her parents finally accepted him, that they are no longer star-crossed lovers.

She runs a finger up his arm and the hair stands up in a sun salutation. "Lunch?" she asks, and they make their way up to the resort, their feet sinking into the sand. At the poolside bar, a group of drunk twenty-somethings argue loudly about the existence of God. The speakers blare soca music as the entertainment team gears up for an afternoon Zumba class and the woman's husband pulls her against him to sway their hips together in time with the beat.

The smell of grilled meat wafts out from underneath a covered tent, a line of people snaking way from it. They stop to deposit their towels at an unmanned booth and stand aside to debate the merits of the various resort buffets.

A shadow swallows them. It is a man, impatient, holding out a balled-up towel. Its corner hangs over his pink wrist like the tail of a domesticated animal. The woman's initial confusion gives way to embarrassment when, in a flash, she remembers what she and her husband look like. She folds in on herself, shrinking under the awning of the booth.

"Do I just give this to you?" The man hands her his towel. His back is sunburned, the shape of a sleeveless genji outlined in relief. The curve of its deep neck grins at them as he walks away.

Don't Lie to Me

Lizz Schumer

I haven't trusted doctors since I was a child. Doctors don't tell you the truth when you're under 18, masking everything in games and ruses meant to distract you from what's really going on. But I've also been an astute, watchful person. Even as a baby, I stared, tracking the world with wide eyes. I sat in the kitchen with the adults instead of playing with the other kids, trying to figure out the world. So when my dentist asked if he could "count my teeth," I wondered what kind of professional doesn't know how many are supposed to be in there.

And when my pediatrician talked about looking for fairies in my ears and my mouth, I said "ah" with skepticism. I knew there were no fairies in there, that there couldn't be, and that made the man with the big nose seem like a quack. "Mom," I wanted to say, "Do you think this guy's legit?"

A nurse practitioner OB-GYN, Mom believed in calling body parts by their names. She didn't go in for the cutesy euphemisms most parents teach their children for their private parts and didn't dumb down the answers to our questions about how our bodies worked. "Your body parts have names," she told my brother Tim and me. "And it's OK to use them." As a result, Tim once walked around his preschool classroom, informing each child of what part they had underneath their clothing. "You have a penis," he told his best male friend. "And you," he proclaimed, turning to a nearby girl, "Have a vagina." The preschool teacher called home and told Mom what had happened. The teacher said Tim had been using "potty talk" with the other kids and that she didn't think it was appropriate.

"Well," Mom said pragmatically. "At least he was using the correct terminology. Can't learn that too early."

So it confused me that, at the offices of the professionals Mom took us to, things weren't nearly so direct. It didn't make sense to me that she believed in calling a spade a spade, or a vagina a vagina, as the case may be, but her colleagues wanted to fly airplanes into our mouths.

§

The first time I realized doctors could hurt me, I was seven or so. Born premature, I had a battery of tests every so often, to make sure I was developing properly. This particular session took place at the big hospital downtown and required a day off of school. That excited me; an entire day with Mom all to myself was a treat, even if I did have to sit through what I expected would be another series of baffling games involving colored blocks, beeping noises through headphones that covered my whole head, tracking lights with my eyes, that sort of thing. I was promised pancakes afterward, and that sold me on the whole adventure.

But this time, the doctor led me into a little darkened room and proceeded to "draw" on my belly with a cold wand. "Look," he said, pointing at a little screen. "I'm making pictures in your insides." The squiggles and lines on the tiny TV fascinated me. I'd never seen anything like it. While I watched the tiny ecosystem of my own body wriggle and dance onscreen, the doctor (or maybe an assistant, I can't remember) plunged a shot into my abdomen. I hadn't been told this was part of the equation and felt wounded by more than the needle.

I've forgotten what that test was for, although I remember refusing to pee on a table later, a catheter insertion that hurt in such an elemental way, it reverberates to this day. I remember another nurse, later on, telling me to look out the window at a pretty-colored car while she drew my blood. While the results of that day have faded in memory, the feeling of being lied to has embedded itself in my very cells. It's a part of me, thrums wetly in my blood and bones.

Afterward, Mom took me to a diner with Formica tabletops and syrup in red plastic ketchup bottles. I squeezed more and more of it onto my pancakes, waiting for her to tell me that's enough. But she didn't, and the sugar prickled my back teeth as I polished off every buzz-inducing bite. There wasn't enough sweetness in the world to salve my spirit, that day. I don't know if the doctors' honesty about what was going on would have made me feel more empowered, more included in my own medical care. But I wish I had the opportunity to find out.

§

As an adult, I know these methods have a reason. Many children can't handle the complicated terminology, frightening complexity of medical procedures. But to me, their games and euphemisms felt like betrayals. Hundreds of tiny misdirections resulted in my deep distrust of the medical establishment, as a whole. If I couldn't rely on them to tell me the truth about why I was there, could I really be expected to trust their diagnoses? As a child, I was a fiercely literal creature and as an adult, I still don't like the way euphemisms shimmer and change, shapeshifting depending on their source and intended target.

My body presents the same, regardless of what we call it.

Faulty

Broken

Invalid

Malfunctioning.

All facts, albeit ones that casts a shadow over the honest parts of people's faces.

Chronically ill: another one, but a more PC version that smells like disinfectant and squeaks like nurses' shoes.

Disabled: somewhere in the middle, acceptable only in contexts that have decided it's so. As a writer, I traffic in words. They wind their way around my misfiring synapses, sparkling in ways that invite, repel understanding depending on the functionality of my particular brain, the unique character of the day. I'm not afraid of calling my body what it is, not after more than 35 years of trying to part the curtains doctors, society, the limitations of language have repeatedly drawn around it. Because euphemisms aren't just confusing; they're a portal to fear. There's a reason horror movies hide the monster in the basement, behind the shower curtain, in dark corners where it can jump out—gotcha! Scream, I dare you. We fear what we don't understand.

Disability isn't anything to be afraid of, and neither are the ways we navigate a world made to keep us in the dark corners where so much of it still believes we belong. These days, when my doctors use words that obscure, I illuminate them. I'm not afraid to drag us all squinting into the sun.

Illness as Metaphor

The Gallbladder Monologues

Kathryn Aldridge-Morris

1. I've got gall. That's what men have told me. *You've got some gall.*

2. The first time a man tells me this, I am eleven. We are straddled across an inflatable banana boat off the coast of Yugoslavia, some time before its body politic implodes, turning in on itself. There are a few families on this banana. He is one of the fathers; the kingpin of the drinking dads, and one of my dad's best new buddies. He smooths his thinning hair, pushes his Aviators onto his head and straightens his pink-burnt back for the official photograph. I laugh out loud. You're on a banana mister, is what I'm thinking. But I've transgressed in a way it'll take me years to understand. *You stupid little cow,* is what this dad says to me—an eleven-year-old with buck teeth, awkward in her school Speedo swimsuit. *You've got some bloody gall.* And then my dad glares at me through his own new Aviators, shaking his head.

3. Gall, or bile, aids digestion. It has also been defined as something bitter to endure. And impudent behaviour. Whatever that is. Hippocrates proposed the theory that there were four humours in the body—blood, yellow bile, black bile and phlegm—and these could determine a person's temperament. Any imbalance could lead to sickness or mental instability. An excess of yellow bile was associated with increased anger or irrational behaviour. Subsequently, bloodletting was very popular throughout Medieval Europe until the 19th century.

4. My symptoms are part of a whole parcel of symptoms first put down to perimenopause. The doctors see a woman 'of a certain age.' Those male doctors of the same certain age; all they see is black bile, yellow bile.

5. Decades after that banana ride, I find myself doubled up in pain in Accident and Emergency. It's biliary pancreatitis. 'You have three gallstones,' the consultant tells me. We're in a little curtained cubicle alongside the overspill waiting area. 'Probably had them for years. We call them *silent stones.*' I am wearing the tote bag I bought in The New York Public Library; **I contain multitudes** printed across it. I reach inside for my diary, make notes as she tells me about my inflamed pancreas, my deranged liver.

6. During my MRI scan a month later, a cannula is inserted into my hand so that the nurse can pump contrastive dye into my abdomen. I lie still as a shaman in my low white cave. The cold spreads inside my insides. I feel like I need to pee. The dye will highlight any complications with my anatomy. How often have men complained I was complicated? That and the gall. Not straightforward like other women, they say. With more gall than you can shake a stick at, the idiom deriving from farmers controlling their sheep with staffs and how it became impossible when there were too many sheep to herd. That's me. A multitude of uncontrollable sheep rampaging through fields of men, shaking their sticks, shaking their fists.

7. My mother had her gallbladder removed when she was my age. She would have been divorced nearly twenty years by then. She told me afterward she'd had an out-of-body experience, floated up to the ceiling and watched herself from above. At my pre-assessment the surgeon explains my abdomen will be pumped full of carbon dioxide during surgery. I want to ask him about out-of-body experiences but figure he won't take me seriously. Instead, I envision myself inflating, a zeppelin the shape of a woman's body, a blimp, an aerial protest.

8. In the three-month wait for surgery, I google everything there is to know about gallbladders. You can eat normally once it's removed but might not process fat as well as before, and you may gain weight. I recall during one of my father's weekly visits, how he once spread out his arms, held them

in the air behind my mother's back and grinned at me. *She's got so fat*, he stage-whispered. I'd looked over at my mother. She was curvy, not fat. *Too wide*, he pronounced and lounged on the orange foam sofa while she prepared his dinner. I still recall the pain in my chest when he laughed as he repeated the word *wide* under his brown-ale breath. The pain was not dissimilar to gallstones, when your organs fail to work in harmony with each other. A feeling of stabbing.

9. *Too wide too fat too loud too aggressive too assertive too unpredictable too passionate too emotional too fiery too angry too temperamental too bolshy too feminist too choleric too much,*

   the fathers, the teachers, the boyfriends, the driving instructors, the tutors, the doctors, the neighbours, the bus drivers, the men wearing Aviators riding inflatable bananas.

10. My Scouse mother had attitude when she was young. One afternoon, swinging her tennis racket on Penny Lane, a Mini had slowed by the curb, four local lads wolf-whistling. She told me she'd said to her friend: 'Oh god, it's The Beatles—don't look at them!' and kept on walking. Then she married a narcissist and learned she had to shrink to survive; herself, her opinions. To not have too much of the old gall or step out of line. She became a silent stone. There was no bile letting, you could say.

11. In 2023 Puffin Books rewrote a number of phrases in Roald Dahl's children's books for its latest print run. The words 'fat' and 'ugly' are removed. Aunt Sponge is no longer 'terrifically fat' or 'tremendously flabby.' She's now a 'nasty old brute.' Hadn't 'fat' after all been shorthand all this time for 'nasty,' for nagging, for women who fell short of men's expectations? Uncompliant. Who had a lot of gall?

12. The women in my family: our rage gathers, accumulates, amasses into a hailstorm of gallstones.

13. How different things could have been if my father had substituted the word 'fat' for something else. Resilient, resourceful, lonely, sad. *How sad she is*, my imaginary father could have said. *How sorry I am.*

14. Somehow it wasn't enough to remove her gallbladder. My mother's body never unlearned how to store the melancholy of black bile. Never had the right conditions. The stigma of divorce in the seventies. The poverty of being a single mother. The knowledge that your best friend was now in your husband's bed.

15. Me? I'll continue to need bile. My body will continue to produce it. But I'll no longer store it, carry it around with me in my gallbladder. Anger and shame—they're like gallbladders: parts of ourselves we don't need to hold onto. This much I've learned.

16. The time has come for surgery. It's been three months since one of my silent stones voiced itself in my bile duct. I'm wheeled to the theatre. The anaesthetist arrives with the surgeon. 'That tickle you came into A&E with?' The surgeon smiles. 'There'll be no more of that after today.' I frown, feel the cannula go into my hand. The anesthetist asks me to count back from ten. I don't. I'm too busy thinking: Did he seriously just use the word 'tickle'?

Valley Fever

Amy Champeau

When I tell people who live in the Sonoran Desert that I had been sick for six months with Valley Fever, they take a deep breath in, then blow it out with a strong sigh. They nod empathically. Invariably they will make a comment about how exhausting Valley Fever is and they will tell me stories— about a construction worker who contracted the disease from blowing dust and had a lung removed; about a woman who never knew she had Valley Fever, only later to develop asthma and lung disease from the nodules which had stayed lodged in her lungs for decades; about relatives who had died or contracted lung cancer or become incapacitated or bedridden as a result of the fungal spores which enter the body through the nose and take up residence in lungs and, worse, the brain. Some people will tell me that a person never fully recovers from Valley Fever; it is always lurking dormant ready to spring out, full-blown, weeks, months or years later. Though Valley Fever is considered rare, some people will say that everyone who lives in this part of the southwest United States is infected with the disease, whether they know it or not. It is part of the lore of this section of the country. They say that it is a sort of initiation, the way the Sonoran Desert welcomes them.

I may have contracted Valley Fever when my husband and I first moved to Tucson from Chicago. Initially it seemed that I had the flu. The first symptoms of Valley Fever are flu-like: cough, headaches, fever, chills, chest pains, fatigue. I waited for the 'flu' symptoms to subside. But the fever of over 102 degrees continued for weeks. Doctors thought I had pneumonia. I was so weak I couldn't walk from my bed to my desk, ten feet away. On a chest x-ray they saw 'something.' So they prescribed antibiotics. But the antibiotics didn't work. I had taken for granted my citizenship in the kingdom of health; I had crossed the border into the kingdom of sick.

For centuries, visionaries and spiritual seekers have gone to the desert to confront questions of life, death and spirit. As early as the fourth century,

Christian monastics instinctively sought the desert in a quest for solitude and retreat from the world. The desert can represent extreme deprivation and harshness as well as impossible survival. The desert can be a place of trial and transition and waiting. The Sonoran Desert where we lived, home to a multitude of species of cacti, roadrunners, snakes and javelinas, was also home to a fungal infection living deep in its soil.

In the soil, the fungus *Coccidioides immitis* grows in fine filaments which degenerate to produce spores. They are so light that any disturbance to the soil—farming, construction, even a gust of wind, as my doctor had suggested—can launch fragments of the fungus into the air. Once airborne, the fungus is carried on tiny particles of dust, which can be inhaled. Inside the human body, the fungus goes through a spectacular metamorphosis, each spore of fungus swelling into a spherule, a round capsule carrying fungal cells. These spherules can rupture, creating more spherules and spreading the fungus throughout the body.

My husband was not happy when I became ill. One weekend afternoon shortly after I got sick, wishing for some comfort and companionship, I asked him if he would sit with me and rub my back. He was standing across the room at the kitchen counter, his back turned to me, shoulders hunched, head bent, poring over some mail he'd brought in from the box out front. Without turning around to look at me or acknowledge me he yelled, "You're not sick; you're making it up." He told me these were detox symptoms from the deep bodywork I received from him and that I was making too much of all this, that I should take hot 'detox baths' of baking soda, sea salt and Epsom salts.

I felt then the familiar sinking in my chest, the contracted sensation as I became smaller—not physically smaller really, but shrunken and younger, my shoulders rounded and pulled forward as if I were a child being scolded by a parent. I felt sicker, and weaker, too, as if my immune system were also shrinking inside my body. I stood there, my back against the stucco wall, feeling its uneven surface prick the skin of my back through the thin fabric of my pink nightshirt, feeling as weak as a newborn kitten, barely able to hold myself upright. I retreated to bed, alone.

While I was trying to figure out what was happening with my body, he went to Los Angeles to celebrate the Japanese *Obon* ceremonies, a Buddhist tradition honoring the spirits of deceased ancestors returning to this world to visit their living relatives. It was while he was away that I received the 'news' via the imaging lab's email that I might have cancer. A follow-up CT scan showed hundreds of 'nodules' in my chest. They told me I likely had 'metastatic disease,' that I had cancer somewhere in my body which had spread to my lungs. The doctors scheduled a lung biopsy.

I called my husband. "I might have lung cancer," I told him over the phone. Silence. Then he said: "I was thinking of leaving you, but now, of course, I won't. We'll get through this."

Well, what could I say to that? You're leaving? Or: I'm glad you're not leaving? Or: When were you going to tell me you were leaving? Or: Can I count on you? Or: You're a fuckin' asshole.

The nodules turned out not to be cancer, and some weeks later, a doctor did a simple blood test and determined that I had been infected with Valley Fever. It was too late for treatment. I would have to wait for time to heal my body. I was still very ill. My previously strong legs could barely carry me from one room to the next. At times exhaustion—one of the most lasting symptoms of Valley Fever—would overcome me, exhaustion so deep it felt as if the floor of life energy was opening up and I was going to be swallowed in the depths of the Earth.

I slowly regained my strength and later scans showed no further nodules or any trace of Valley Fever. I recovered completely. My marriage, though, did not recover. Our relationship remained as prickly as the Saguaro cacti outside our door.

My therapist and my friends had been telling me for months that my husband's behavior was abusive. They pointed out that the way he spoke to me, criticized me, controlled our finances, refused to listen to me, how he threatened to leave me when I was sick and refused to support my need for medical attention were hallmarks of partner psychological trauma. I didn't want to believe them, didn't want to admit it to them or to myself, but in a deeply knowing part of my being I knew it was true.

My denial was not unusual. Like Valley Fever, psychological intimate partner abuse is difficult to detect, even though it has existed behind closed doors for millennia. It can lie dormant for years. Bright, articulate professional women like many of my clients, women who have worked hard to become successful doctors, professors, veterinarians, psychotherapists—refuse to believe in psychological abuse. They tell me it couldn't be abuse because their partner doesn't hurt them physically. Instead of setting limits and boundaries, speaking up and finding their voices they try harder to make their relationships successful. Like Valley Fever, psychological abuse takes time to diagnose, can be debilitating, and recovery can take a long time. The scars, though invisible, can last much longer than the relationship itself.

In the most deadly outcome of Valley Fever, the fungus reaches the brain and patients require anti-fungal treatment for life. Similarly, the most lasting thing about psychological abuse is how it gets into the victim's mind. Emotional violence changes you at a cellular, mental level. For a long time, my brain was 'infected' with my husband's voice, telling me who I was and how I was and how I should be. With therapy and support and education, his voice in my brain has quieted. Sometimes I hear my own voice inside my own head talking back to him now, saying, "See? Look how great I'm doing. See? I'm writing. I have love in my life. I don't need you." I look at the mountains surrounding Tucson and the white clouds in the always-blue sky and marvel that I have survived.

Separated from the Body

Holy Hour

Amanda Leigh Lichtenstein

1.

A whole hour. On my hands and knees. Drenched in sweat. Swaying on a wooden floor. Before I heard the voice.

Return to your body, it said. *It's OK now to return.*

The voice told me to grab the rope. The rope was my breath. I climbed my breath out of this animal-like state, knot by knot, to the surface of myself.

I blinked several times until a pair of legs came into focus. And then I remembered it was Saturday. I was in Indiana, at my boyfriend's house. A self—my self—was slithering back to the present.

"How long have I been like this?" I asked the legs.

"About an hour," the man attached to the legs said.

"An hour?" I repeated, incredulous.

A hijacking. A possession. A trance.

How did I even get here? I remember lying on the couch, clutching at an ember burning in my chest. I remember wailing in fits and starts—trying to let out a howl. And then I couldn't breathe. Nothing to remember after that.

A stolen hour—gone.

I looked down and saw that I was nearly naked— my shirt had been tossed half-way across the room. My boobs had slid half-way out of my sports bra. I sniffed my armpits, pickled with fear. I sat up on my knees, lifted a tingling hand and dragged it across my chest, slick with sweat. And then my hand wandered up to my head to feel my hair matted in swirls against my forehead.

I was a feral beast trying to recall her life as a human.

My boyfriend looked like a cardboard cutout. I squeezed his calves for confirmation of life. He held out a warm towel for me to wipe down my face and chest.

"Take your time," he said. "You're OK."

I dressed slowly and wandered to the couch to stare off into the void I had just occupied.

Then I recognized a feeling I knew: hunger. *Hunger is so beautiful.* My first full thought. I realized I had to speak those words to be heard.

"I feel like maybe I died," I said. "I'm so hungry."

"I'll take you to get enchiladas," he said.

Sitting in a tiny orange booth at Don Andres, I stared beyond the dying plants on the windowsill into the twinkle of lights in the dark night. I felt myself trying to return to the storied world—one where a beautiful man with blue eyes was sitting across from me, talking about food.

I called up the script to match the moment: restaurant scene.

Almost there, the voice said. *Keep going.*

I scanned for signs of recognition. Clocked the ice-cold Mineragua glass bottles standing in rigid rows at attention in the cooler, the sizzle and grease of grilled meat. And then I glimpsed my reflection in the window—a self with silver hair pulled up in a messy, high bun, staring back at me.

Our food arrived like an offering. I watched my boyfriend plunge a fork and knife into his overstuffed burrito drenched in green salsa, taking in one enormous bit after another with great enthusiasm. And I took in the miracle of his face.

At first bite of enchilada smothered in sour cream and oily red salsa returned me to the world—me and my body—as willing participants, once again.

We want to be here—and so we are.

2.

I've spent years trying to manage my mind's wild impulse to flee my body. But this time felt different—I had never heard that voice come through so clearly to rescue me.

My therapist asked me on our regular FaceTime call what might have triggered the panic attack. That's what most people call them, and anyone who's ever had one usually gets asked this question.

But the truth is that there's no specific trigger for the eviction—and certainly no notice. Even the slightest hint of threat can rally the body to kick out the mind and by the time I notice, it's too late. I'm already riding the express train to a dispossessed state.

That morning, hours before that ember in my chest began to glow so bright I thought it'd burn a hole through me, my boyfriend and I were lazing around in bed, swapping stories about our childhoods.

I stumbled upon memories of Holly, a girl with greasy long hair that clung to the sides of her moon-shaped, pimple-pocked face. She smelled like the inside of a rabbit cage. She liked to sing constantly in the highest pitch but just below her breath, in her own little world. No one liked Holly. And I worried even then that I saw parts of Holly in myself.

I remembered going to her 10th birthday party, a small group of us sitting around a circular table in her cramped kitchen on a cold spring day, eating potato chips out of plastic bowls. Holly flitted in and out of her bedroom to show us her half-dressed Barbie dolls, one by one. Her parents were both very kind, disheveled and slow-talking people who blasted us with rotted breath every time they spoke too close to our faces.

That day, Holly and I sat in piles of dirty clothes on her bedroom floor, playing Barbies for what felt like way too long. I remember wanting to be rescued. I wondered if my absentminded father, always lost in a jazz tune, would remember to pick me up. I knew that my mother was too depressed to pick me up from anywhere. No one could be trusted. And it seemed to me that Holly's parents needed parents. Holly was an orphan.

My little heart swelled with quiet pride that I had volunteered to be her friend. But in those excruciating hours that went by on her bedroom floor, I must have disappeared inside myself, because I don't remember anything else about that day.

Back at school, I continued to protect and defend Holly against anyone who tried to mock her high-pitched singing or told her she had zits. We lost touch after elementary school. I never heard from her again. I learned later that she had married an Orthodox Jewish man and slipped into another self.

Nothing about our brief friendship had caused me any knowable pain. But soon after my mind called up these memories that morning—I disappeared into the void.

Hijacked. Possessed. A stolen hour.

And then I heard that voice—coaxing me back into the present.

3.

I am no stranger to these sudden waves of terror. When they come, I medicate to mute the struggle and wait—twenty minutes or so—until mind and body decide to conspire again—and I'm back, as if I'd never left.

I've abandoned myself in many places over the years—on buses in foreign countries, in hotel beds with bad lovers, in traffic jams on the highway, on my bedroom floor during a workday. Each time I return, I carry the fear of a future burn.

As Kierkegaard once said, anxiety is a school; I am a lifelong student of its rigorous curriculum. I have learned, over the years, to study my body for subtle signs and hints of hijack.

But I had never been so far gone that I needed a voice to call me back home to my body. This time, I spiraled through a portal that led me to this version of myself—one who understood more clearly how the body has its own mind—determined to unbuckle itself from the muck.

Perhaps time spent in the hologram of Holly's kitchen had sparked my body's revolt against remembering a deep grief—that I, too, was a neglected, disheveled little girl. But once the body decides to eject the mind—or the mind decides to escape the body—the original wound no longer matters.

That hour on my hands and knees on the floor felt like a century of supplication. My sweat, the smoky balm in the makeshift body church of an unnamed hurt.

In the weeks after I heard that voice—the one that told me my breath was a rope I could tug and climb back to the surface of myself—I started listening for it everywhere.

It felt like the voice of a mother calling her sobbing child home. (I was the mother, I was the child.) It felt like the voice of an angel, the one who, according to Talmudic scholars, leans over each blade of grass and whispers, "Grow, grow." (I was the grass, I was the angel.)

I used to dread these moments when my mind packed her bags with intent to flee—a refugee from reality. But this time, she returned with a souvenir—the gift of clarity. I was in awe. Now I know that this kind of leaving and returning is a prayer.

Cold Case Files

James Montgomery

On 28/09/1995, at approximately 3pm, I responded to a homicide report at 19 Cedar Way. The body was a 7-year-old boy. There was no blood, but the right wrist had been twisted, so the hand lay limp at an odd angle. I was told by the mother they had been shopping in town. The boy squeezed her hand to cross a road, when the boy's father snapped, 'He's too old for all that.' This makes the father the prime suspect, but he has an alibi—always has an alibi—because he's never truly there.

On 9/05/2001, at approximately 11am, I responded to a homicide report at Willow Croft. The body was a 13-year-old boy. There was no blood, but the mother found him surrounded by 12 silver-foiled packs of mouldy sandwiches. I interviewed the boy's friend. On most days, he said, the boy would throw the sandwiches away, feeding them to the same hungry bin at the back of school. If the boy forgot, they would be hidden in a wicker basket in his room. The boy told the friend the dizziness was a kind of adrenaline. After his mother discovered the uneaten sandwiches, the boy bought a card to say sorry. This makes the mother the prime suspect, but she swears she only ever wanted her son to eat.

On 17/07/2004, at approximately 7:30pm, I responded to a second homicide report at Willow Croft. The body was a 16-year-old-boy. There was no blood, but a toothbrush was clamped in the boy's right hand. His mouth frothed with toothpaste. Forensics discovered the boy's gums had been rubbed raw. A 25-year-old male revealed he had been intimate with the boy in a parked car a while earlier, sometime between 6-6:30pm. This would make the 25-year-old the prime suspect, but the law says 16 is the age of consent, so technically the man had committed no crime.

On 1/3/2009, at approximately 3am, I responded to a homicide report at 38 Dallas Road. The body was a 21-year-old man. There was no blood, but the man was wearing a homemade Peter Pan outfit. The man was severely underweight. An autopsy detected significant levels of blood alcohol concentration. There was a rumour that, on the night of the death, the devil had visited the man. If reports are to be believed, this would make the devil himself the prime suspect, but I deal with cold hard truths, not sin or lost boys or pirates with missing hands.

On 4/11/2013, at approximately 5pm, I responded to a homicide report at 148 Watermarque Apartments. The body was a 25-year-old man. There was no blood, but the man sat up and said he couldn't even bear to be touched, so what use was his body?

On 18/03/2023, at approximately 10:30am, I responded to a homicide report where I live. There was no blood, nor a body—only an empty house. I sat at my desk with the weight of my thoughts. Inviting them in, coaxing them close, holding them tight.

The Head That Almost Floated Away

Jane Palmer

Butterfly

I opened my eyes to see tattooed bodies staring at me. The buzzing of machines had stopped, and I was on the floor of the studio. My tattoo artist helped me up and gave me some hard candy to suck on. Butterscotch, just like my grandma always had in a little bowl by her favorite chair.

"You fainted. You have to remember to breathe, Jane. Wait, you didn't have lunch today, did you?" she asked, clearly concerned.

I thought for a moment and looked at my watch. "Oh shit. No, I didn't. Can I come back another day? I promise to have a big meal beforehand."

She nodded and, as she wrapped up the partially completed rainbow butterfly on my upper back, she said, "You're welcome any time."

I wasn't skipping meals, at least not intentionally like many other 19-year-old girls I knew. I just tended to forget to do important things—like eating or breathing.

I was a butterfly, flying from place to place, with no safe spot to land.

Labyrinth

I became a floating head after I was raped. Before the rape, 13-year-old me had a body. A body with skinned knees and freckles and scars. Before the rape, 13-year-old me dated a boy who stopped when I asked. After the rape, I wore an armor of XXL clothes on my small frame. After the rape, I was a balloon on a string floating from one place to the next.

As a floating head I was really good at *thinking*. I would escape into books, a dreamy intellectual space where no one could harm me. But I missed *feeling*—pain and pleasure. Whether it was during a tattoo or sex, I'd watch myself from above unable to feel what my body was experiencing.

Lost in a labyrinth, I was unable to find my way back to my center.

Compass Rose

In my early 20s, about ten years after the rape, my body revolted.

I was unwilling to admit my back spasms were alarm calls—each spasm was like the Whos in Whoville yelling "We are here!" I tried to quiet the Whos with pills and alcohol. But they were so damn loud. And I started running out of doctors who would prescribe more pain killers and muscle relaxers.

But I could *feel* again. I could feel my back tighten and seize. I could feel the lightning bolt down my spine. I could feel the floor against my face when I was unable to lift myself up. I could feel the pounding headache and sour stomach after a night of too much whiskey.

At the time I was a social worker working with clients who were survivors of sexual assault. I wanted to understand how trauma gets trapped in the body, so I attended a somatic experiencing training. During a practice exercise, I burst into tears—snot-everywhere sobbing. I-had-to-run-and-hide-in-the-bathroom sobbing.

The instructor found me and said: "I didn't realize you were still a floating head. You have work to do, my dear."

The Whos really needed my attention. But I refused. I moved to a new city, found new doctors who would prescribe pills, and continued to try to quiet the Whos for ten more years.

I had my map with a compass rose. I knew what direction I needed to go, but I couldn't see clearly how to get there.

Phoenix

One night, in my early 30s, I was out for drinks with an old friend.

"What would it be like if I became the kind of person who did yoga, meditated, and quit drinking?" I asked.

"You wouldn't be Jane." She replied.

This was true, but not my truth. I aspired to be that person, but I couldn't admit it. And I didn't know how to start. Laughing, I told her she was right and ordered another drink.

Soon after, a back doctor offered to start giving me injections in my spine for pain relief. I didn't take him up on his offer. I'd have to drive 40 minutes each way for the shots, and driving exacerbated my pain. I was too busy as a full-time Ph.D. student and part-time graduate assistant. And I was so tired of doctors and pain medicine. I was ready to try something new.

There was a Hatha yoga studio near my apartment offering a $35 per month unlimited class pass for students. My supervisor knew I struggled with chronic pain and convinced me to sign up for the pass. She told me she'd treat my 9 am yoga class twice a week as physical therapy appointments and expect to see me at 10:30 am on those days.

For the first time in my life, someone had given me permission to take care of me. It is fucking hard to learn how to take care of yourself, especially after two decades as a floating head. I cried during hip openers. I fell over during tree pose and triangle. But after six months of yoga, my pain was gone. The Whos were quiet. I no longer needed pills to get through the day.

I was a phoenix, finally starting to rise from the ashes.

Typewriter

I had my body back. My floating head was reattached to a beautiful, strong body. I began to rediscover pleasure and pain. I could stay in my body during orgasm, instead of floating away to the corner of the room. When I got a tattoo, I could feel the needle on my skin. I started writing again. After decades of being unable to write a word, I was writing every chance I could.

I had my body back, but I was still so afraid. I instinctively cataloged all the exits in any room I was in. I couldn't sit with my back to any door. I wouldn't take the elevator. I wouldn't take a taxi by myself. I stood in the back at concerts. I avoided tunnels if possible.

Talk therapy wasn't helping. I was too good at over-intellectualizing. I realized I was finally ready for body work. I found a somatic experiencing therapist who pushed me to notice the sensations in my body. I still cried, but in a good cathartic way, instead of the running-and-hiding-with-snot-all-over-my-face cries. I joined a meditation group. I slowed down and paid attention to my breath, my steps, my words, and my actions. I took writing classes.

I had a story to tell.

Tortoise and the Hare

In my late 30s, when I was trying to get pregnant, my doctor suggested I try acupuncture.

"Jane, you're killing yourself," my acupuncturist said.

"I am? How?" I replied, unsure how she could know this on our first visit.

"You mentioned you're a trauma survivor. I can tell your sympathetic nervous system is activated."

"What does that mean?"

"You're stuck in fight-flight mode. You've probably been stuck there since you were 13. I doubt you're going to get pregnant before you learn to activate your parasympathetic nervous system." She looked at my confused face and said, "What I mean is: you have to learn to relax."

I laughed. "I don't relax. I work all the time. I don't watch TV. I don't read for pleasure. When I go to the beach with my partner and her family, I stay inside and work on my laptop. I can't just sit on the beach all day."

"If you want a baby, and want to live long enough to see a grandchild, find a way to relax."

I was a hare who had to learn to be a tortoise.

Twins Constellation

About a year after I started going to acupuncture, I became pregnant with twins. I was still trying to tame the hare into being more like the tortoise. The pregnancy was high risk, so I spent much of it on bed rest. The head that almost floated away was attached to a body that was growing two humans. I could feel them inside me. I watched my belly begin to look a tortoise shell.

The twins gave me permission to take rest seriously.

Anatomical Heart with Seedlings

"You came prepared!" my tattoo artist said, as I took protein bars and coconut water out of my bag. We were taking a break halfway through a four-hour appointment.

"Oh yeah, I fainted during a tattoo like 25 years ago. I never want that to happen again!" I replied.

"Yeah, protein and hydration help a lot. You also just have to remember to breathe." She said.

"I've gotten a lot better at that over the years." I said, smiling.

Postscript—People often ask me about the significance of my tattoos. They are my passport stamps, forever etched on my body, as I found my way back to me.

Voice and Movement

Wendy L. Parman

Voice and Movement class for actors. Four semesters, starting sophomore year, at the University of Kansas. Marcia Grund, our instructor, was small and square, with chin-length reddish-brown hair that stuck to her sweaty freckled face. She told us her spine had been fused as a teenager due to a serious automobile accident and was in a body cast for a long time. Pain darted across my body as I listened to her story. She had a dance background. Her healing was created in the fires of suffering, learning, teaching others.

It was a challenging class where we were trained in a variety of physical and vocal disciplines. I was uncomfortable in my body, anti-athletic. Still, I appreciated the subtlety of the Linklater work, the quiet adjustments of the Alexander work. Other approaches brought extreme visceral responses, especially for me, or so it seemed. And she had us journaling.

Sometimes Marcia gave us strange "body" assignments, which we'd reflect on in those journals. One assignment was to go home, strip naked, and put a paper bag over our head. Eye holes were to be cut out, so we could see just our bodies in a full-length mirror without our faces.

I had three roommates at the time, none of whom were in theater or the arts. They were all friends of my first roommate, Sheila, whom I'd been paired with freshman year. They were from moneyed families in the suburbs of Chicago, with names like Winnetka and Lake Forest, places I could only imagine. They went to frat parties, dressed in button down preppie shirts, or dresses by Laura Ashley. I stayed home from parties, dressed in my only pair of jeans and my dead uncle's plaid shirts from the early 60's, rummaged from the back of some closet.

The only full-length mirror in our apartment was in the hallway, between the bathroom and the bedrooms. This seemed a recipe for disaster, since Sheila and her crew were hanging in the living room, watching television. Sheila and I were bona fide friends. She had a more tolerant attitude toward my quirky creative traits than most of her crowd. But she wasn't above teasing. In fact, she wasn't above cruelty, a thing I'd witnessed, though usually directed elsewhere.

"You have to do what?" Sheila said, after I explained my assignment. "A paper bag? Oh my gaaaawwwwwd that is hysteeeericaaaaallll."

"Yeah it's kinda weird. Um, but I have to do it, so, um, if you guys would just stay out of the hallway for like, I dunno, 10 minutes? I'll be quick. Just leave me alone—ok?"

"Oh," they said most sincerely. "Of *course*. We're watching *Dallas* anyway," Sheila condescendingly reassured me. "You do your weird theater thing."

I seriously considered not doing the assignment at all or lying about it. I could cheat and *pretend* that I had done it. I can make shit up with the best of them. But I really did not want to rob myself of these experiences, even if some of them were downright miserable. I assumed there was something of value to be found in this exercise. And I was nothing if not a trouper. This is the number one lesson you get as a young person in the theater. You do the job, whatever it is. You toe the line. You show up, on time, prepared, committed, ready to go. Suppress your outrage, your confusion, your fears. Do it.

So, I did it. I got the paper bag. I cut out the eye holes. I disrobed hesitantly. I gingerly crept out into the hallway, looking both ways wide-eyed. I crept to the mirror, hoping against all reasonable doubt that they would, mercifully, leave me be.

This might be the place to mention that Sheila's favorite toy was a Polaroid camera.

I wasn't there for more than 5 seconds before *** FLASH*** and again ***FLASH FLASH*** loud hysterics, jumping up and down, pounding of high fives all around. The body attached to the paper bag head bolted at the first flash. Hyena haws continued as the Polaroids slowly came into focus.

"Give me the fucking pictures," I seethed, once my body was shielded in the safety of clothing.

"I couldn't heeeelp it, it was just too weieieieierd." Sheila's blue-grey eyes twinkled like a child caught in minor mischief.

FUCK YOU, SHEILA! Door SLAM!

I sat on my bed behind that slammed door, clutching a pillow. The steam of shame that had built up in me threatened to give way to the torrential tears behind them. At the same time, I was willing that NOBODY better DARE WALK THROUGH THAT DOOR. In a bit, Sheila poked her head in, tossing the Polaroids on the bed.

"I'm sorry. We're going to the Jayhawk so you can do your 'assignment.' We'll be out all evening."

I glared, silently sub-texting, "You better fucking be, you heinous bitch."

I could hear quiet giggles and Sheila shushing her soon-to-have-business-degrees friends out the door, with a quiet click. Warily, I emerged from the room, and opened the front door. The hallway out to the elevator was empty. The living room was still. I searched the other bedroom, just in case—even the closet. They were gone. I went back to the front door and latched the chain lock so they couldn't get in if they did come back.

Stark naked in the too brightly lit hallway, a body stood in front of the mirror, the head covered with a paper bag with peepholes cut out. I was looking at someone else's body. It was different than I thought it was, bony at the elbows, the collar bone, the knees. The hip bones protruded slightly. The body was rounded in the expected places, but in the brutal glare of harsh appraisal and agitation there was nothing sexy about it. Slouched shoulders, also bony and crooked, one side noticeably lower than the other. There was something sad about the way the body held itself, as if in hiding, afraid. It had none of the qualities of beauty I had sometimes imagined I possessed. Was this the body that men had made lecherous comments about as I went from rail thin to having womanly curves, comments that made me wish my body would disappear?

A twisted knot of dizzying sensations whorled inside of me, along with a vague nausea, as I struggled to hold my gaze on the image in the mirror. At last, I tore my focus away, running back to my room, as if other's eyes, both imagined, and remembered, were burning through me. I ripped the bag from my head and began to dutifully write in my journal. All of it. All the dysphoria, all the wishing my body away.

When Marcia handed back our journals, she had written in the margins her concern about my experience. Maybe I wouldn't have had such a disconnected, critical appraisal of my corporal image had it not been for the shaming provided by my gleeful "friends." I imagined this exercise was designed to help us see our bodies more objectively, less harshly. But I had had the opposite experience. The truth is, this exterior that housed me had been objectified, idealized, shamed, and abused from a young age, by various members of my immediate family, something I had no real understanding of yet. The mirror, the paper bag, the naked body, and the Polaroid all landed me right back in that wound, a wound so familiar to so many women. But I would not identify any such wound for years to come. I was just weird ... off. Something was terribly wrong with me. And whatever it was, I had to hide it.

It Wasn't Supposed to Be Like This

Kim Ruehl

I sat on the edge of my cozy, impossible-to-leave bed and stared through the window at the squirrels as they peeled bark off the young redwood in our backyard. For their nests, their babies.

Beyond them was a small wood, thick with leafy, green summer trees that blocked any view of the sky. The squirrels gathered, stockpiled, built, as the young man on the other side of the phone explained that the metal rods attached to my spine during scoliosis surgery thirty-something years ago were going to now prevent me from being "awake" when my son was born.

My son.

Six years ago, a doctor in a comfortable office chair leaned forward at his desk and told me there was less than a five-percent chance I would ever get pregnant. "I wouldn't waste your money on IUI," was a sentence he uttered to me. Then: "Have you been having hot flashes?"

We'd charged ahead, trying to get my wife pregnant again. She'd endured somewhere around a dozen miscarriages as I stood by, helpless and longing, providing support, whatever that meant. Then suddenly stars aligned: the new doctor, the inheritance, the fibroidectomy, the donor egg, the last vial of sperm from the same donor we'd used to make our daughter, the kismet of the stranger in the UK, who offered the vial free of charge. "If you handle the bureaucracy of getting it shipped to America," she'd written in a private message on the sperm bank's website, "it's yours."

One IVF was all it took to get my "don't waste your money" body to hold onto a pregnancy. The new doctor cried when he called to tell me it was a boy. He knew how long we'd been trying, how badly I wanted this.

Now, someone who didn't know anything about this journey was telling me I would need to be unconscious for the birth. He was not the first person to tell me this. The doctor who performed the surgery on my child body in the 1980s had informed my child face that I would probably not be able to get an epidural, should I grow up to become someone's mother.

Only weak women get epidurals, I thought at the age of 12. *And I am going to be a strong woman.*

Now, I was an actual 43-year-old woman, watching squirrels like they could do anything to change my situation.

Seven weeks after the positive pregnancy test, just as I was beginning to experience some moments that weren't shrouded by nausea and hormonal moodiness, I entered Covid lockdown. My days were suddenly consumed by managing our kindergartener's circle time on Google Meet.

In a tiny world deep inside my body, a tiny embryo we made from a donor's egg grew from the size of a lentil to the size of a kidney bean to the size of a kiwi. Meanwhile, in the outside world, literally thousands of people were dying from an unknown, incurable virus every day. My wife, the Family Medicine doctor, continued to see patients, while our daughter and I stayed home for months, while my belly grew and the quickening came and the clothes stopped fitting and my sleep became fitful.

I read the news and avoided the news and spoke to almost no adults outside of my household, aside from my doctors, throughout my pregnancy. My therapist told me that crying releases tension in the nervous system, so I set aside time each day to cry. To wonder: Have I yet become that strong woman?

"But when you wake up, you'll have a baby," the voice on the other end of the phone was telling me.

What the actual fuck is life right now, the voice on the inside of me said.

And then, eyes still fixed on the squirrels—nobody was going to put them to sleep when they were giving birth—I breathed in through my nose and out through my mouth and resigned to the lack of control I had over absolutely anything anymore.

The morning I checked into the hospital, as numerous people tried to shove an IV line into my hand, a different anesthesiologist entered the room. "I see you're planning general anesthesia. I'm wondering: Can I at least try a spinal? I'm pretty good."

"Yes," I'd told him. "Of course. Absolutely. Please."

I was moved into the operating room and told to sit on the table, bend over forward. I parted the gown and felt as though someone quickly touched my skin with the tip of a paperclip.

A woman I've never seen before comes out of nowhere to tell me to swing my legs onto the table and scoot down and lay back. That I have about fifteen seconds to do this before I lose all sensation from the chest down. I scoot down the table faster than I've ever done anything.

Almost immediately, my body begins to shake, which I'm told is normal. I'm not cold but they pile me with blankets and I'm grateful for the extra weight. Sandbags tethering my hot air balloon to earth.

I hear another woman's voice asking who my favorite singer is. *Patty Griffin*, I tell her, and suddenly Patty Griffin's voice is in the room. "She flies through the air with the greatest of ease," she sings, "just over there on the old trapeze."

A moment later, another woman appears: the surgeon, who went to residency with my wife. They are on a first name basis. They have inside jokes and a secret language, as all doctors do. It's heavy on abbreviations and polysyllabic words with very simple definitions.

She tells me she's going to begin the procedure, as someone I've never seen before rapidly, urgently erects a paper wall that allows me to see the surgeon but almost nothing else.

I can tell from the surgeon's shoulders that her hands are moving quickly. She tells me I'll feel pressure in just a moment, and then I feel like someone is pressing on someone else's body, and then there is some strange indication of release, and then someone holds up the body of a small human infant that I simultaneously don't recognize and also know deeply, instantly. He appears to be smeared in mayonnaise and pissed all the way off, and he looks at me like "Wha—?" and I cry.

The surgeon asks me if I'm OK. My wife asks me if I'm OK. All I can do is shake my head and nod because I both am and am not OK.

There is my son.

My supposedly hopeless uterus turned an invisible cluster of cells into that person right there, with toes and fingers and nostrils and a blue tube protruding from his belly. That umbilicus will shrivel and dry and fall off and I will place it in a small baggie, knowing I will never look at it again but also knowing I can't possibly discard any piece of this little, impossible person.

We go home and, for the next few months, I am back in the dull grey hum. Everything makes me angry. Everything is hopeless. I am a failure, a waste, a burdensome blob who is the worst thing in everyone's life. Nobody says the words "postpartum depression" to me because everyone is a little depressed during lockdown. The way I feel maybe makes sense to everyone else, somehow.

The world is stretching in disconnection, everyone reaching out for hands and grasping only foggy, muddy air. The future is uncertain, but isn't that always true?

One day I fall onto the bed, where my wife has placed our son while she brushes her teeth. He locks eyes with me as I cry. I see his crystal-clear, blue, brand-new infant eyes studying the face of this person to whom he feels indelibly tied, not remembering that he used to live inside this body that now appears so full of despair.

His glance is searching and full of love and full of sadness and full of longing and full of fullness. And for the first time in months, I feel truly awake. I feel my hair on my face and my toes in my socks. I am seen by another human. I wipe my eyes and kiss his tiny face and tell him, "Mama is OK. Mama is going to be OK."

Layers

Melissa Flores Anderson

She slipped on one layer of wicking cotton, then another layer of form-fitting spandex, then a down vest, to fend off the cold. This time of morning, when no one else was awake yet, she moved her limbs briskly toward the orange light coming up over the tree line in the distance east of her home.

She took a photo of the sun haloing over the tree line, golden and red hues streaming out from a center orb. She knew the photograph could never capture the brilliance of seeing it live. She posted the picture online and watched to see who would like it. She was only interested in one person's response, but she knew he would never give her that heart she craved.

That night, from three thousand miles away, he posted a sunset with brilliant pinks and purples. Pink at night, sailor's delight. She liked it as she liked all his posts. But this one felt different, like a silent siren call to her, a reminder that they watched the same sun in the sky even if they were separated by the wide breadth of a continent.

She thought she could keep him on a separate layer, like a photoshop project. One layer, the life where she took that daily walk at sunrise, where her toddler pulled at her clothes all day long, and her husband wrapped around her body at night on the second story of a sprawling house that was always too hot or too cold.

And on this other layer, the insomnia she suffered months into the pandemic and after the wildfire alerts started. The whole world felt ablaze and it seemed silly not to confess that once, once long ago there had been feelings for that man on the other coast. On this layer hidden underneath a polished veneer sat the secret conversations with this faraway man, where they flirted and reminisced about an old, almost relationship they'd had together. In the quiet hours, when he didn't have to look her in the eyes and had no fear of rejection as he knew she was married, he said he could picture them dating. If she were single now. He said their timing was always off.

But she knew, it was never just the time. It was the separate space they occupied in the world and the way they moved through it. She stayed in place and watched others leave. She held onto every bit of people, all the conversations and interactions swirling in her head, like a riptide of memories and nostalgia. He collected destinations and discarded people, like old chewing gum.

They had started with chewing gum, when she carried that green and red wrapped pack in her pocket, the smell of artificial watermelon matching the taste of watermelon lip smacker on her lips. She slipped him a piece after class and they blew bubbles with it, popped them and laughed. They were kids then. Babies, really. Before anyone had broken their hearts or broken their spirits. Before they kissed for the first time and had drunken sex ten years out of high school. Before he ghosted her the first time.

She tried to write him out of her system, but the feedback always came back critical. From editors. From writing partners. "I don't get what the MC sees in this guy. Why give him a second chance? What's the attraction?"

She couldn't explain that when they were twelve, he was so far out of her league and the fact that he wanted her then, bound them together. But even that wasn't the truth.

There was another layer, one hidden and closed off, that she rarely let herself glimpse.

The truth was that she heard for so long from all corners of the world that her body was unattractive, undesirable, unfit to touch, unfit to love. The breasts that came in before the end of elementary school and sagged in the cheap elastic band bras from the local department store, the hips and ass that couldn't fit into a pair of Guess jeans, the thick eyebrows that earned her the name Oscar the Grouch in home economics, the acne that dotted her back through high school. She came to understand that men would only touch her when they were drunk enough to have an excuse for it.

She couldn't even trust the man she married when he said he found her attractive. He'd met her when she was thinner. When she starved herself and ran five miles a day to get down to a size 14. He proposed to a false version of her body.

But the man on the other coast, he'd known her for three decades and he'd wanted her in all her iterations. That was the attraction she couldn't quite express in the stories—that need for someone to want her physically and not despite her physicality, to tell her that her body deserved to exist in the world.

Because underneath that layer was the layer that she tried to erase and never could. The one that was fuzzy and unclear except where it was sharp and raw. The trailer in the backyard of the old house. The attic. The dirty magazines. The bush that hollowed out in the middle like a jungle gym. The hidden places where she couldn't hide her flat chest and her skinny legs, where she couldn't push away the hands and the tongue and the body parts she didn't dare name. She'd learned before she knew what desire was that it was a shameful thing, a violent thing, something to fight against.

She tries to build more layers. The professional self. The calm and collected blazer-wearing, eyelash-curling, mascara-sporting communications professional who holds it together in a crisis. Who makes sound decisions with a moment's notice. Who understands the nuances of politics, gains the trust of executives, hits all her deadlines. This layer stoic and strong and well put together. Until that meeting where someone brings a dog. Not a therapy dog, but a Canine Companion. They will assist officers with supporting victims. A deputy district attorney starts to talk about how the dogs will sit with children on the stand who face abusers. Mostly sexual assault. And she feels the layer start to crumple and she focuses on a clock on the wall to hold it together.

The lawyers leave behind a beanie baby version of the dog and her boss gives it to her to take home to her son.

She thought she could keep the layers separate, but they are all built one on top of the other, precarious and unstable. The first layer runs vertical and defies distance and time. It shrinks and becomes invisible only to explode and splatter across her life. She doesn't know how to contain it.

On the drive home, she turns up the volume on the songs in her car and cries as she drives along the farm road between the office and her house. By the time she is home, her face is dry and she smiles widely. She sheds the layers of clothing she wears, the blazer, a knit sweater under it, the knee-high boots and stands in a holey camisole that shows a spot of her belly through it. She hugs her son and hands him the stuffed dog.

Another layer starts to form.

Growing Older

Flesh. Wisdom. Crone.

Sue Zueger

Now:

She finds an inch-long whisker sprouting, playing the banjo on her chin. She swears the previous day there was none. Last week, while peeing, she plucked two white hairs from her nether regions, not that it's well-traversed territory any longer, so she shouldn't care. Still, who needs a reminder of the weeds that need tending over her nearly six-foot acreage. Her tits, the ones that barely filled size 34 A cups, spill out the sides of their 36 B hovels. She is a sausage in Spanx. A banished queen, hiding bags of coin behind her back, an ogress with an attitude, a troll with a temper and an ass to match.

Then:

She doesn't know her loveliness. Standing in front of a mirror, she pulls the skin from each thigh so there is gap, a great abyss into nothingness. She wants to erase the strong legs that run miles. She wants blonde, wants short, wants notice, wants a junior high standard of beauty.

Now:

Her wedding dress, the first one: him, her. Black Irish, they say. Are they brother and sister, they say. So much alike with their dark hair, white skin, blue eyes. A dress that still hangs in the closet, still can't give it away. It's a reminder of her little soul, the one that couldn't speak in full sentences. A reminder of how she now knows how to parse the syntax of life, even if she doesn't fit in the damn dress anymore. She shows their daughter, lets her try it on, thankful when the miles of buttons won't catch.

Then:

A fourteen-year-old who teeters on heels in a pew at the wedding of some relative. At the reception, her uncle's friends approach her thinking she is older (or do they), their whiskey-scented mustaches, their leering eyes, their hands on her upper arms. Then she doesn't know that beauty is an invitation. She doesn't know "Leave me alone."

Then:

A first-year teacher, a school resource officer sits in her room while she reads aloud. He crosses his arms in the far back. She doesn't know it isn't normal to be visited by anyone, let alone a school resource officer. At first, his eyes rest a little too long on her and then shift to the nubile girls, the ones who don't change out of their gym shorts before her class. She interrupts his sight line, stands near their desks, ruins his view. He stops haunting her and the ones in her charge.

Now:

She can't fit her hand between the waistband of her jeans. She visits her hairdresser monthly to hide the gray. She winces when she snaps her fingers. Everything, everything, every little thing aches. She doesn't like her face in the reflection of a morning mirror, the store glass, the rear view. When did she become old? When did she have to reconsider the next size up? But, god, she loves her mouth, her brain, her come-on-mutha-fucka-I-dare-you.

Missing The Tampon Window

Melissa Llanes Brownlee

I say I am so tired, my body doesn't do the things I know it could. I bend down to pick things up and my back laughs at me. I run on the treadmill and my heart can't wait to jump out of my chest, needing to lounge in a beach chair, sipping a caipirinha. My arms flap when I point at something, the ubiquitous bingo wings, swinging. My eyes fry in the UV light of the day, my stubborn ass not wanting to admit I need glasses, no matter how cute they are now. I say getting old can really suck, my uterus finally deciding it's done producing, blood leaking on everything when I miss my tampon window.

My husband says you are so tired. I see your body can't do the things you think it should. You bend down to pick things up and your back laughs, I hear it. You run on the treadmill and I know your heart can't wait to jump out of your chest, hoping for a caipirinha and beach chair beside some distant ocean we can't reach. Your arms flap when you point at something, I would never call them bingo wings and I curse the day you learned about them from your Aussie co-worker. You need glasses and sunglasses. I keep telling you this but you don't listen. You say getting old can really suck, and I hear ya. Your uterus may be done trying to make babies, and I am sorry you missed your tampon window. Tampons, really suck, don't they?

Forty-Six

G Lev Baumel

I was forty-six when I found out I was pregnant for the second time in my life. At thirty-two, doctors had let me know with certainty that I probably would not be able to get pregnant at all, but should that happen, my body would most definitely not carry a child full term.

When I was thirty-three, my daughter was conceived naturally. She gestated for thirty-nine weeks and five days and arrived in her own time, in a birth pool, in the bedroom that would have been hers, had we stayed in England. Her name means Life in Spanish and Heart in Hebrew in honor of different parts of her heritage; later on, I learned that her middle name also means Lion.

As soon as my daughter was born, people started asking about the next child. Instead, we moved to New York, and then California where her father and I split amicably. Today, we are both happily married to other people.

Over the years, my child occasionally requested a sibling. I responded honestly that between the divorce and the years chugging along, the clock inside me had run its course.

§

At forty-six, I attributed my newfound aversions and exhaustion to the elusive catch-all for women my age: perimenopause. My husband suggested I take a pregnancy test after I told him for the umpteenth time that I was feeling *off.* I laughed but didn't protest when he volunteered to drive six miles to the pharmacy to pick one up.

I laughed again, a hysterical gurgle that swelled up from somewhere I couldn't touch, when the little word *pregnant* appeared once, and then again, and again: four different sticks all declared the same thing. My husband's reaction was similar - "No way," he said before doubling over with laughter. We hugged and took selfies holding up the little stick so we could one day show our child how happy we were at learning the news.

That week, I told my daughter that she might become an older sister. It probably would have been more prudent to wait, but I wanted to explain why I had been acting strangely.

Upon hearing the news, my twelve-year-old sobbed. She was worried about bringing about even more changes beyond Covid, moving in with her stepfather and three step-siblings, and the three dogs, two tortoises, the bearded dragon, and twelve chickens, that had been added to our single pup and two cats. I held her tight, protective of all that already existed, yet hopeful about what was growing inside me. My daughter looked at me through her tears and asked, "what if you die?"

She wasn't the only one: people's reactions were very different at forty-six than they had been at thirty-four when the congratulations and excitement were rarely tempered. At thirty-four, my fears were met with waves of the hand and affirmations of "you're strong," and "it'll all be fine." At forty-six, there was shock, urges to remain "cautiously optimistic," and encouragement to "stay positive." I peed on stick after stick in the hopes of finding reassurance in that one little word. Still, no matter how often it appeared, I was not convinced that I was actually, really, truly *pregnant*. My mind continued to tie itself in knots, while my body felt luscious, delicious, and alive, as if I should be growing my chin-length hair down my back, plunging my feet into wet soil, and painting my face with mud and fresh clay from the river bottom.

§

I found myself simultaneously preparing for two divergent next chapters: one where my child-rearing years soon came to a close. In this scenario, my husband and I would find our home empty of children and the constant demands of pick-ups, drop offs, play dates, and parent conferences within about six years. Simultaneously, I was now also preparing for the arrival of new life — an added bonus round. My confused hormones were having a party.

It was hard to picture parenting a toddler at my age: walking them into pre-school, my husband's white hair, my salt-and-pepper, looking like everyone else's grandparents. Nevertheless, I was giddy at the idea of sharing a biological child with my second husband, creating a biological bond between his children and mine. I hadn't known this baby was possible and I wanted it so badly. There was nothing to do but want; I couldn't change what nature had in mind any more than I had planned to get pregnant at forty-six.

§

It is the night before Thanksgiving and my husband and I are preparing to host nineteen people, when my twelve-year-old runs into the kitchen. She jumps up and down in front of us: "Uh, Mamma, can you come please?" She rushes back towards the bathroom, slams the door behind us, locks it, and then lowers her pants to show me the blood in her underwear.

Unlike my generation, my daughter and her friends talk openly about these things. Before today, as the last in her friend-group to get her period, my daughter was growing desperate. Today, it has finally, finally come.

I demonstrate how to attach a pad. This time it isn't in case, as it was in July before sleep-away camp. Now it's real.

"Do you want to learn how to use a tampon?" I ask.

She shakes her head, "not yet."

When I got my period, around the same age, I was on vacation in Buenos with my father who was squeamish about anything girl-related. He sent me out alone to find a pharmacy in a strange country, to request things I knew nothing about, in a language that wasn't mine. Even in English, I'm not sure I would have known what to request.

My daughter emerges from the bathroom within a few minutes and proclaims herself "A Woman" to her fourteen-year-old step-brother who wrinkles his nose without looking up from his video game. I am relieved that while everything has changed, everything has, thankfully, also remained the same.

§

The following day, my husband and I gather with our former spouses, their new partners, a few friends, and all the kids, around our makeshift table. My daughter sits straight up, beaming: "It's strange to think I've become a woman." She mentions this a few times over the course of the weekend with equal amounts bashfulness and pride, curiosity and trepidation. I check on her throughout the days and nights, like when she was a baby.

"Cramps suck," she says.

I nod and hug her.

What I keep to myself is that on the same night my daughter started her very first cycle, I also started bleeding. She had been anticipating what I had been dreading—the site of blood in my underwear.

Over the next few days, I text and call different medical professionals. They have all kinds of caveats: what color is the blood? Is it cloudy or clotted? Despite my desire to have the right kind of blood, what is happening is happening.

§

I bleed for twenty-five days. One night, I bury the tiny membrane that comes out of me under some rocks in front of my office at three-thirty in the morning, in the rain. The next day, my husband laments that he wishes he had been there too. I am sorry to have excluded him, but also relieved to have done it by myself. Unlike my daughter, who has grown into mine and her dad's and her own person in her own world, this tiny being still feels like mine alone.

§

When I got my first period at age twelve, I told none of my friends. I never did learn who started first, which one of us bled last. My daughter, on the other hand, triumphantly texted her group chat, who congratulated and commiserated with her on entering the world of cramps, cravings, and blood. One of her friends, who is a year older, and who recently changed pronouns from she/her to they/them, gifted my child (she/her), a period bag. On the front, a large sparkling eye is stitched for protection, and inside her friend crammed tampons and pads of every size. My daughter and I shared pads for the first time the weekend of Thanksgiving. A few months earlier, she started borrowing my clothes, and then my shoes. Slowly, I regained my body: my breasts shrank back to their regular size, my moods stabilized, and I was able to stay awake past seven-thirty.

§

I loved being pregnant both times. The second one reminded me of how much I enjoyed the first. Unlike the first, however, when my second pregnancy ended in miscarriage, because I was forty-six, I knew there would be no trying again, no next time.

Living Waters

Sandell Morse

In Siracusa, Italy, I followed a guide down centuries worn, narrow, curving uneven stone steps to a recently uncovered (1989) *mikveh*, ritual bath. Nina, my 19-year-old granddaughter walked behind me. Nina is the daughter of a Korean, Buddhist, now Christian mother, and a Jewish American father, my son. Mostly, her Judaism has consisted of attending Passover Seders and lighting Hanukkah candles. I was surprised she knew what a *mikveh* was. At her age, I hadn't a clue—or maybe, I had. Perhaps, a distant notion of an ancient practice or perhaps a practice that belonged to Orthodox women who wore wigs or head coverings, dark dresses, dark stockings, and lace up shoes. These women immersed to purify before returning to the marital bed. Those purification customs, the *mikveh*, had never belonged to me, a child raised by a fiercely assimilated Reform German Jewish father; a young woman who married an equally assimilated Reform Jewish man.

Down, down, down we climbed, our bare arms brushing ancient damp stone walls, the soles of our shoes rocking inside impressions in each step. Water dripped, its sound almost sinister as if we were entering a dungeon. In a way we were. This *mikveh* was the oldest in Europe dating from the Sixth Century BCE, and it had been in constant use until the Inquisition when King Ferdinand of Spain expelled all Jews from his territories.

"None were killed here," our guide said. "They knew, so they left for Turkey, Greece, Morocco."

A soothing myth.

Before Royal officials granted the Jews permission to leave, they appraised and packed their belongings, then gave their possessions to wealthy Catholics. At that time, about 100,000 Jews lived in Sicily. Those who remained were forced to convert, and Jewish culture disappeared from the island. This had been the Church's goal—make the Jews disappear. For centuries no one knew about this buried *mikveh*.

When Amalia Daniele, a Sicilian noble woman, bought a crumbling *Palazzo* in the *Guidecca*, Jewish Quarter, she had no idea the *Palazzo* stood on the site of a buried *mikveh*. Nor did she know the nearby church of Saint Filippo the Apostle, built by the Brotherhood of St. Filippo in 1742, stood on the site of an ancient synagogue. As she renovated, Amalia Daniele noticed odd building patterns, and because she was alert to the ancient history of the *Guidecca*, she researched old records. For centuries Christians had unknowingly prayed to Jesus on the site of an ancient synagogue and an ancient *mikveh*.

At the bottom of the steps, I stood at the edge of three ancient pools. Water dripped. Time and moisture seeped through these walls, and something dormant inside of me awakened. I felt the spirits of those long dead Jews. I was surprised. I didn't believe in the ritualistic laws of purification for women, isolation during menstruation, followed by three days of immersion and cleansing. I eschewed all Jewish law and ritual that deemed women unclean and/ or subordinate to men. Yet, thinking of the men and women who had bathed here, then been forced to leave their homes and the lives they'd created or convert to a faith that was not theirs, moved me and I felt the tug of our common history.

§

Four years later, I stood on a stone step inside *Mayim Hayyim*, a *mikveh* and learning center in Newton, Massachusetts. I'd removed nail polish, contact lenses, hearing aids, all jewelry. I'd shampooed my hair, cleansed my body, every crevasse, every pore. I was naked, as naked as the day I came into this world.

My life had undergone seismic shifts since I visited the *mikveh* in Siracusa with Nina: a house sold, an apartment in a retirement community for my husband, a condo for me and Zeus, my Standard Poodle, in a nearby town, a life apart after nearly sixty years of sharing houses, a pandemic, isolation, fear, depression. I continued to write, publish, hike, ski, and care for Zeus. I was living alone—my choice; yet, at eighty-three, I felt as if something was missing inside of me. I had entered the final passageway of my life. I could tuck into my shell or celebrate with renewed strength.

I took a deep breath, left the last step, and immersed in the *mikveh*. I was celebrating the taking of a Hebrew name, Sarah, and my renewed commitment to whatever lay ahead. The pool was a perfect size and shape to embrace my body, the water a comfortable ninety-five degrees. I spread my arms. The water entered every pore of my body, soaked my hair, touched every scar. I loved this feeling of nearly floating under water, and I stayed until I needed air. I recited a blessing in Hebrew printed, transliterated, and attached to tiles above my head. In my prayer, I honored the Holy One for these living waters. I was doubtful about God, and as I spoke, my throat thickened. I stood for a moment and felt my own presence. I was comfortable inside my body, inside my skin.

I immersed two more times, and before each immersion, I celebrated the blessings of my life. I honored those who had helped me along the way and gave thanks for the supportive presence of friends and family and for my life's journey which brought me to this present moment. I thanked the Holy One, the One I did and did not believe in, for the miracles of everyday life, family, friends, and the good I have known. I was grateful for my capacity for continued growth and transformation.

I sank slowly. My body softened. I thought of the Jews of Siracusa, the crumbling synagogue, the church that replaced it, the *mikveh* below, all of it surfacing. When I emerged, I recited the *shehecheyanu*, a favorite prayer thanking that elusive Holy One for giving me life, sustaining me, and bringing me to this joyous moment. This was a prayer I recited when I hiked and gazed out at mountains, a prayer I recited at my Bat Mitzvah at age seventy-two, a prayer I recited inside this *mikveh*, a prayer that linked me to the ancient Jews of Siracusa.

That evening I walked Zeus through the coastal New Hampshire city where I lived. The light was both fading and luminescent. In a park, water bubbled and cascaded in a fountain. Flowers bloomed, impatiens, zinnias, cala lilies, and dahlias. Lime green potato vines trailed, all sparking from within. I sat on a bench with Zeus and watched passersby. How many knew what a *mikveh* was? How many knew its origins? John, the Baptist, was a Jew, a child, a boy, a man, who had known ritual waters. Healing, cleansing, and transforming waters belonged to all three Abrahamic traditions, Judaism, Christianity and Islam, their source the *mikveh*.

§

A breeze touched my arm. I hadn't realized my hand was resting on Zeus's head or my fingers were slowly kneading his fur. I shifted. He rose. I rose. We walked along the edge of the park, then into the South End with its narrow streets and eighteenth-century houses. The night was starry. Beautiful. I was grateful to be alive. I whispered Abraham's word to God, God's word to Moses: *Heneini*. Here I am. Present. Counted. Comfortable in my skin.

What We Do to Heal

Heart and Soul

Elizabeth Fletcher

It came out of nowhere, my galloping heartbeat. I'd been sitting in my pajamas working on a freelance project when it started. I moved to the couch to try to meditate, but the pizzicato beat and cinching of my chest proved too distracting. Instead, I consulted Dr. Google. Since there was no chest pain and I could breathe, I was assured it was probably nothing serious. At thirty-five, I was athletic and in otherwise good health. I stayed put and took steady sips of air until my heart tired of racing—nearly an hour later. But that wouldn't be the end of it. My heart would continue to sprint at sporadic, unexpected moments, along with a growing sensation of a bird fluttering in my ribcage.

§

"Mike," I called to my husband, "Can you come here?"

My heart was pounding again, the first time this happened when I wasn't home alone.

My husband worked in the cardiac medical device industry and knew more about the workings of the heart than the average Mike. He placed his fingers on my carotid, "Oh my God, you're tachycardic. I have to take you to the hospital."

I pushed off his suggestion. First, because I dreaded the fuss—perhaps a trait of being a woman, a Minnesotan, or a potentially fatal combination of the two. But the other reason was because I believed it would be pointless. I was ignorant that the codeword "heart" would grant one a fast-pass to an EKG, instead envisioning an expensive, hours-long wait in the ER by which time my heart would be tapping nonchalantly like everything was fine.

"I can't let you return to Guatemala if your heart is doing this."

My next trip was months away, and I wasn't about to up and cancel for no good reason. I had been invited to study with Guatemalan daykeepers—something that brought out epic eyerolls in my STEM-oriented partner. I gave him the side eye, unsure if he was looking for a reason to tank my trip.

"You have to promise to go the doctor."

"I will."

"No—you have to *promise* me you'll make an appointment on Monday."

I put my hands up in surrender. "I promise."

§

The forty-something cardiologist with a III behind his name arrived in a crisp white shirt and onyx cufflinks to discuss the findings of the echocardiogram and Holter monitor, captured weeks earlier. He spent the first fifteen minutes of my consult talking about his snowy commute, Mike and I giving each other occasional WTF eyes, before he finally got down to my case.

My EKG had scribbled out a picture-perfect sinus rhythm. Bloodwork: normal with electrolytes in perfect balance. The echo showed no physical anomalies, though even I had witnessed my rogue, off-tempo heart valve on screen.

The 48-hour Holter monitor documented around 5,000 extra heartbeats each day called premature ventricular contractions—the reason for the fluttering bird that now beat its wings almost constantly. But it had failed to catch the more unpredictable supraventricular tachycardia, or SVTs. The PVCs, or heart flutters, weren't an issue, but the SVTs could cause cardiac arrest or lead to heart failure over time. The cardiologist could not say what triggered these arrhythmias so suddenly.

"This started two weeks after my last trip to Guatemala," I said, as I'd told every doctor I'd seen since Mike had insisted. The timing felt like a critical detail. An American doctor we'd met in Guatemala hosted medical conferences on tropical parasites, and I thought exposure to some foreign bug might be the key to unlocking what was happening inside my ribcage. The cardiologist shrugged me off, writing a prescription for beta blockers that I could use during an episode. I accepted the slip from him, dissatisfied.

§

In the three years since I'd fallen in love with Guatemala, I'd been shown a different way of seeing the world, of astral planes and subtle energies. Which is why, two months after meeting with the cardiologist, I was sitting in the hallway outside the healing room of an indigenous curandera I'll call Violeta, Mike waiting for me in her house's attached garden. She and her brother-in-law Alberto, a powerful healer in his own right, sat across from me. My American vagabond friend, living with Violeta's family while apprenticing with Alberto, acted as my translator.

While I'd wanted a ceremony with Violeta for the sake of experiencing one, it had not occurred to me until that moment to say anything about my arrhythmias. I had thought, perhaps, that returning to Guatemala might end them, but nearly four weeks after my arrival, they continued on as before. Perhaps Violeta would know how to cure me. I had nothing to lose.

I described the electrical storms of my heart, about the bird fluttering to get out of the cage of my chest, about the cardiologist's diagnosis. Violeta and Alberto asked about my stress. I shrugged, nothing extraordinary.

Violeta spoke, "During your last trip, you opened to sacred energy. But you left space for another energy that does not belong. Your body now holds two energies that are not compatible. They are causing problems with your heart."

Violeta's words clicked as the face of a fellow traveler I'd crossed paths with the summer before flashed to mind. Drama and chaos seemed to swirl around this person. Each interaction, however brief, left me off-kilter and needing a few hours to metabolize what I could only describe as their sticky energy. I suddenly recalled this person talking of their own heart arrhythmias.

I'd been so naively open then, so unprotected, as I explored Maya spiritual practices that my subtle energy body—the animating life force radiating from my physical self—had picked up an energetic contagion that was wreaking havoc on my physical body. In an instant, the connection between body, mind, and spirit came into sharp focus, the lens through which I saw the world opening wider. How I'd need to strengthen my own filter rather than act as a human satellite dish picking up everyone else's energy.

I stepped into the healing room, sunlight spilling through the window, where Alberto would work with me first. A small shrine stood in the otherwise empty room—one white candle flickering in front of several framed images of the Virgin Mary. My friend pointed me to the center, explaining that Alberto was a midnight shaman. So named because he was occasionally called out in the night to the scene of a susto—an accident, injury or fright that could cause a person's soul to fragment and provoke illness. He could retrieve a sick person's lost vital energy and return them to health.

Supine on the white tile, its coolness seeped through my shirt. Alberto gathered a glass of water, a short, knotted rope. I closed my eyes as Alberto splashed water on the floor around me. He spoke in Spanish, then Tzutujil, his velvety voice hardening. My eyes jolted open by a sudden crack next to my body. My friend put his hand on my arm and encouraged me to relax. I trusted that I would not be harmed, so I closed my eyes once again, sensing Alberto circling my body. The gusts of his movements washing over my skin. The violent cracks of his whip built to a climax. Followed by a span of silken silence. Alberto and my friend blew a powerful breath over my crown. Then my heart. Then my hips, knees, feet, shoulders, and hands. Returning my soul back to me. Alberto placed the whip in my hands, the course fibers tickling my skin. Distant birdsong filled my ears. For the moment, the bird in my chest stilled.

Alberto and my friend slipped out when Violeta entered. She instructed me to remove my shirt and bra. A small bundle was attached to her index and middle finger that, presumably, contained healing herbs. Maternal and tender, Violeta ran the bundle in long, fluid motions from my navel to fingertips. I had nothing else in my adult experience to compare to the deep sense of safety, to her soft strength.

She ended the healing by saying, "It has been a pleasure. Your energy is light and clear."

I felt light and clear as I dressed. A million things I wanted to ask and say as Violeta waited with me, but my fledgling Spanish held my tongue captive.

When we appeared in the garden, Mike shot me a look, eyebrows raised.

Translation: "I can't believe you left me with these crazies."

Together, we walked to the ferry docks as I told him what happened.

"I think they're quacks," Mike said.

"I know that's what you think."

"There's no magic."

"But there is."

I smiled and squeezed his hand, knowing we'd never agree. Neither of us aware that the bird in my chest had permanently taken flight.

Walking . . . Meditation

Ellen Birkett Morris

I spent years ignoring my body, ignoring the tightness in my calves from cerebral palsy, ignoring a limp from surgery that left me always slightly off balance. I walked quickly down hallways (just to get it over with) and across broken pavement, falling occasionally.

When I was young there was no penalty for this disconnection. It was so easy to pretend that nothing was going on, that sometimes other people wouldn't notice my limp. This gave me a kind of perverse satisfaction, the cognitive dissonance of having passed for normal tinged with the shame of hiding an important aspect of who I am and what I endure.

When I hit my mid-thirties all of this changed. Arthritis had set in from walking with an uncorrected gait, and undiagnosed rheumatoid arthritis left me with roving joint and muscle pain. I went to physical therapy, did hot soaks, and used braces, pain patches and pain reliever.

All of that helped, but it did nothing to address the mental fatigue and worry that came with a body that was always clamoring for my attention. On the advice of a friend, I tried a meditation class that met in small Unitarian church that managed to be both run down and beautiful.

We sat in a small circle, eyes closed, breathing, while I noticed the outdoor sounds. Birds sang and lawnmowers buzzed as I tried to focus on my breath. Sometimes I would sneak glances at the others just to see if they might be looking back at me. A writer of fiction, I would find myself weaving stories about their lives. But, I had yet to find my mind/body connection.

Then we tried a walking meditation. We lined up in our sock feet with the instructions to feel every part of the process. I put one foot in front of the other, arms out for balance, willing myself to slow down. I felt my feet against the cool floor, the push against the ball of my foot as I stepped forward, the firmness with which my heel landed.

As I walked, I recalled the slap of my feet on the floor of the doctor's office as I took my first steps after surgery. I was a child then and motivated to reach the doctor, whom I knew would reach into his pocket and hand me some gum.

This time, I felt the wonder of every step, this act I used to rush through. One foot after another, I walked past dusty pews as the evening light shown through the stained glass windows, mindful of my movement, for once at home within myself.

Flying

Terry Opalek

I land like a lopsided pony, my left foot hitting the shiny floor with a whack. As it echoes down the long, locker-lined hallways, heads quickly turn. Everyone is laughing. *I'll never get this right. I'm such a dork.*

Skipping is close to flying. For a brief moment, if you get it just right—you are free. It's not an easy thing to do, although everyone in my 4th grade class can. Everyone but me. But I won't give up. I've got one side of my skip working.

I embarrass easily. When teachers call out my name for attendance and oral book reports, my face heats up like a hot plate, turning deep red all the way to the tips of my ears. The rushing blood fills my head, and I can't hear anything but my pounding heart.

To avoid the embarrassment of my lopsided skipping, I try to find a quieter place to practice, somewhere less crowded. Today I go to the school library, where the hushed voices and silent stacks of books make it nearly the perfect place. The sun shining through the large windows lights the maple-colored wood floors. The long open space from the main door to the far side of the room gives me what feels like miles of space—to fly. It's against the rules to be loud or disruptive. I take my chances anyway.

I start with a half-skip on my right side. That side is easy. I'm stuck on the left side. Up I go in the air on my right and then a clumpy landing on my left. Right up… left up - stomp. Right up… left up - plop. Right, flight. Left, stomp. *Come on! You can do it!* Right—flight, left—clomp. *Pick it up!*

Suddenly it happens. Once. For a brief moment, I'm in the air on one side and then the other! Then a clumsy plop. The kids in the library have turned in their chairs and are watching me. A few of them giggle. My face starts to heat up. Other kids smile. They look happy for me.

I'm in the middle of my runway and I know it's *do or die*. This feels like the right time. UP-joy. UP-smiles. UP-flying.

I'm flying across the library, picking up speed and heading toward the sun. Grinning ear-to-ear, my face is glowing red, but I don't care. I am flying! I am free!

Terence! The librarian whisper-shouts at me.

Grounded. But the joy stays. Bubbling in my belly. I skip all the way home from school that day…and the next…and the next.

Outlasting Angie

Ann Kathryn Kelly

My mother said I was four when I woke one morning with my left eye crossed toward my nose.

"You'd gone to bed the night before just fine," Mom remembered. "Your father and I had no idea how or why it happened."

It seems I was delighted by seeing two of my dog, Happy Doodle, run around the yard. One Happy Doodle had always been a welcome sight, as I'd hug her neck tight and plant kisses on her silky ears. Two Happy Doodles was a bonus, an exciting development I shared with my mother who did not agree with me that it was the best thing to happen, ever.

My parents took me to an eye doctor who spent eighteen months trying to correct my double vision with glasses. Adjustment in the prescription strength, he kept assuring us, was all that was required to correct the problem. We ended up with three pairs: blue oval, brown rectangular, and pink cat-eye frames. In photos, I looked sassy in my pink cats but my eye was still crossed. My parents gave up on that doctor and his rotating inventory of eyeglasses and tried another who was able to correct my crossed eye with surgery when I was six.

I keep a wallet-size photo from kindergarten class picture day in an envelope in my bureau. I'm wearing a sunshine-yellow shirt silkscreened with a laughing cartoon turtle, and my blue glasses. My right eye looks straight into the camera, my left eye looks at my nose, and I'm missing a front tooth.

I look happy.

§

My limp showed up in grade school, afflicting my left leg. My thigh and calf were underdeveloped, and I had trouble flexing my ankle. Instead of pointing my toes skyward when walking and landing on the heel, lifting again on the ball to complete my stride, I swung my left hip out. *Slap … slap … slap.* My foot fell like a pancake to the ground.

My right side, because it worked harder, had noticeably more developed muscles. Our family doctor theorized that I was entering a growth spurt and suggested my right leg might be longer than my left. He recommended a customized hard plastic lift for my shoe. The only thing it delivered was a bill to my parents and a sore heel to me.

My parents next consulted with orthopedic surgeons. X-rays were ordered; my left thigh, calf, and foot muscles were manipulated. They studied my ankle rotation. Stuck small round electrodes to me, while a technician shocked me to chart muscle responses. It felt like someone was pushing cigarette butts into my skin. When he peeled off the nodes forty-five minutes later, I had red welts traveling to my thigh. The detour shed little light on why I limped, and I left the room with what looked like chickenpox.

Questions abounded, but answers evaded. Was it scoliosis? A torn tendon? An inner ear issue impacting my balance? We never received a definitive answer. Being raised in the 1970s into the mid-1980s, MRIs weren't common, at least in my small town. I would get my first one in the late 1990s.

Years would pass before I learned that what I had from grade school into adulthood was called "foot drop." I found the definition on the internet in 2009, as I struggled to understand why I was, quite literally and suddenly, falling apart that summer. I'd been seeing several specialists in Boston for severe headaches that soon turned into skull-crushing ones, along with lethargy, nonstop hiccupping, and dry-heaving among other rapid-onset issues. I was supplementing my doctor appointments with my own Google-fueled research. My limp had gotten bad enough to put me in a leg brace. I read that muscle atrophy often accompanies foot drop, along with lack of balance, toe dragging, knee-locking, and something called "high steppage gait." I'd had them all—for years—but had adapted and gotten on with life. I'd compensated for my toe dragging by hiking my left thigh and hip, as if climbing stairs: high steppage gait. The toe box on each of my left shoes was scuffed, and for as long as I can remember, jeans and pants have been baggier on my left side.

Foot drop is a neuromuscular disorder, tending to affect one foot more so than both. Some people have pain with it, a burning or tingling. Lower back injury can cause foot drop, something like a herniated disc, but so can diabetes, Parkinson's disease, multiple sclerosis. Foot drop often develops after someone has a stroke.

A brain tumor, too, can cause it.

§

A headache pulsated behind my eyebrow as I sat in an exam room on a stifling day in July of 2009. A neurosurgeon had just told my brother and me that I had a cavernous angioma. A brain tumor. It was on my brain stem.

Cavernous angiomas, being neurovascular, have a tendency to bleed. The surgeon explained that some patients, if their bleeds are infrequent and small enough, may only experience short-term symptoms. Then there are those patients, like me, who have repeated bleeds over a period of years, sometimes decades, that produce noticeable and sustained deficits: headaches being the most common complaint, but also double vision in some instances, slurred speech at times. Weakness or numbness in arms or legs, balance problems, or gait disturbance.

Awareness coursed through me like a lightning bolt. *That's me!* Finally understanding *why* was not a relief, per se, but strangely satisfying. I had my answer at last. In time—not that day in the exam room as my mind swirled with new medical phrases and frightening data points—but soon after, I started calling my cavernous angioma "Angie." The nickname made what I had sound less clinical. Less threatening. It was easier to tell friends and coworkers that Angie, not some disease with a long name, was behind my declining vitality.

Angie is close to my given name: Ann. Family and friends call me Annie. Angie was yin to my yang, a realization that, hours and days later as I sifted through what I'd been told, echoed like a gong that's been struck. When the surgeon told me that afternoon it was likely I'd had my cavernous angioma since birth, I inwardly scoffed. Since *birth?* Yet, when I allowed myself to absorb what I'd heard, it made sense. I realized I was who I was *because* of Angie. Despite her. Angie was my limp. My lifetime of headaches. My nonstop hiccups. My crossed eye decades earlier, my dry heaves, my poor circulation that made one foot and leg perpetually ice-cold.

Angie was … me. Two sides of the same coin.

Three Boston neurosurgeons agreed I needed surgery, given my angioma's repeated hemorrhages. On October 6, 2009, after nearly twelve hours of open-head surgery, my angioma with its network of blood vessels was cut from the delicate folds of my brain. I spent nearly a month in a brain injury rehabilitation hospital before returning home for another month of outpatient therapy.

In the years since, I reengaged with life, returned to fulltime work, began traveling again. When I think about who I am today, without Angie, I can answer that I'm healthier. Grateful for what I have and am able to do, while knowing and honoring that the person I am remains shaped by a lifetime with my angioma that I personified.

I've told family and friends that I outlasted Angie. Yet, *have* I? Technically, yes, but I feel what Angie left behind. It's subtle, like a soft tap on the shoulder.

Remember me?

It comes when I get vertigo in the supermarket as I crane my neck to look at the top shelf, scanning too fast across rows of cereal boxes. When I'm brushing my teeth. As I lift my head from the sink after rinsing, my neck will occasionally release a pop. It's always where the neurosurgeon cut into me, where I now have a piece of metal mesh layered over my skull. The pop is fleeting, a mere second, but it radiates a tingling deep into my scalp. The shadow of Angie is there, once again.

I've been told my cavernous angioma is unlikely to come back, yet I continue getting scans every few years, to be sure. When the banging, lights, and vibrations start in the MRI machine, it brings it all back. The pain I was in, the relentless headaches that made me sick across every inch of my body. The fear. I return for the peace of mind that comes with retracing those steps.

My stomach relaxes each time I walk out of the exam room with another all-clear assessment.

Angie was integral to who I was for forty years. She remains in my mind. Though unable now to take from me everything I've built and love about who I am and where I'm going next, she is with me, nonetheless.

Some part of her always will be.

Parched

Tracy Rothschild Lynch

Jen's long blonde hair waves back and forth over my foot, which she cradles in her hands. A plastic basin of water rests, wobbly, on the bed. Jen holds a washcloth of pure white. Hospital-grade, wet roughness. The water is warm, and the room is quiet. No need for words, only the gentle lap of the water as my dear friend dips the cloth, rubs my foot, dips the cloth.

I am in the step-up unit in the hospital on day four of my official, bona fide fight with cancer. My breasts are gone, and I am here, bathed in white: blanket, gown, towels at the foot of my bed. White bandages wrapped taut around my upper torso. In the midst of the white sea is an angry red, clawing its way out of the bandages and toward my neck—this, along with a fainting episode that left me exposing my bare bum to the entire third floor, has landed me in the fancy-pants ward so I can receive the care I need.

At my feet, Jen stands and does the only thing she knows how to do after a friend's routine double mastectomy turns anything but routine. She asked to wash my feet and I relented, opening myself up to any form of detoxification that came my way.

The water's rhythm is a lullaby, and I close my eyes.

§

In my childhood home, my dad's aquarium commanded a place of honor.

Centerpiece of the family room, it emitted quiet gurgles and surreal light, both of which regularly drew me to the mammoth of a tank. Decades before I had ever heard the term mindfulness, I would pull up a chair and watch, soothed by positively everything about it. Its very pace captured my attention for minutes that piled up to hours. During my dad's "salt-water" phases, the display was riveting, colorful as a carnival against the 1970s browns of our paneling, carpet, and furniture.

Candy-colored fish hid among glo-green plastic plants, whose leaves and branches stretched and swayed, stretched and swayed. The fish zoomed, plunged, taunted each other in ways that reminded me of the elementary school playground. And then they rested, floating. Watching them ride the invisible current (pumped in from some man-made intervention under the rocks) bathed me in tranquility. In "fresh water" phases, the mollies were always my favorite. When they stopped flitting their gills and bobbed, I swear I could feel my stomach flip as I was lifted along with them.

There was no such thing as chaos in front of the tank. Sometimes my little sister, Sarah, would join me. She'd pull up a chair next to mine and sit so close our thighs touched. Her feet didn't reach the floor like mine, so she would swing her legs and kick. Swing and kick, swing and kick. Feet tucked inside dusty Keds, we'd swim with the fish for hours.

§

When Jen finishes, she dries my feet with sandpapery roughness. Heels, toes, soles. She gives each foot a squeeze, perhaps to remind me I am still alive and she is still there.

I had been bobbing, light as a molly. Now I watch as she squirts a dab of lotion in her hands, rubs them together musically, and fills the air with peppermint. I inhale and hold my breath as long as I can. She caresses, smoothing the liquid into my skin. One foot, then the next.

They say Jesus knelt alongside his disciples and washed their feet before their final meal together. Muslims wash the feet as part of the ritual of purity. It is respect. It is humility, this giving oneself up to something else. As my dear friend continues, I don't think about any of that, though. My thoughts swim slowly in the basin: this symbol of sisterhood, this sweet moment of timelessness, these quiet breaths—they let me surrender.

I am as vulnerable as the remnants of a sweet dream threatening to disappear with each breath of a new morning.

And yet. The surprise tumor they found, that slippery little sucker tucked tightly within tendons and nerves in my upper left chest, won't stop its haunting. It resided right under the flesh that flames red now, and I hope the doctor—one mere human facing an ocean of cancer cells—got it all out.

§

The black mollies—so black they reflected blues and purples iridescently—were my favorite. The longer I stared at them the more they morphed, their scales feathers. Watching, their feathers would lengthen, and they'd dive and dip gracefully. I found myself wishing my pasty, freckly flesh could convert to feathers.

It was easy to tell when the mollies were pregnant. Their bellies swelled with little round nubs that both sent us running to find Dad and initiated our vigils. Dad would prepare the special holding tank—a small, clear box with upper and lower halves divided by a holed membrane. When the mother molly eventually birthed her babies, they fell to the bottom half through holes big enough for them, but too small for their mother. The tiny holes fascinated me. To be so new and delicate.

"Dad," I lamented the first time he showed me how the box worked, "Don't they want to be near their mother?"

"Yes, but she'll eat them," he explained while toying with pipes and tank supplies aplenty, not even turning around to see my horror. "The holes let them slip to the lower part. That keeps them safe, away from their mother until they're big enough to survive on their own."

Sarah and I would talk about the box sometimes, about how awful it would be to have to live on our own.

We never talked about being protected from our mother. Sitting close, swimming in the serenity of the man-made sea in front of us, we understood those babies were safe.

§

Today I am 53. There's an entire lifeforce under my flesh, and that planet has faced its typhoons. My pancreas gave out forty-four years ago; my thyroid later followed suit. My retinas balked at having two pregnancies close together, so they tried to darken, but doctors, lasers, and I fought back.

Cancer procured my breasts, but underneath I discovered strong ribs and proud posture. And although my heart stopped once, twice, four times, it was only crying for help; a sturdy pacemaker now keeps watch. Each organ, vein, nerve, bone, muscle a fighter, a soldier tall and brave. All of me held together by flesh that opens its pores readily to drink up a warm foot bath from a friend.

I sense a history of love trembling in my arteries, millennia of lapping waves. It sounds an awful lot like awakening. This is how parched soil must feel as thunder rumbles in the distance.

And yet. I never washed my sister's feet. Not once in the years that amassed. Not one of the thirty days she spent in the hospital dying. I couldn't see her like that, mind, organs, and flesh destroyed by acts originally of her own making.

Sarah swam around and around in circles for so long and so hard. Furiously, she darted, searching for her life. But the pools she chose to swill were too toxic, our mother's addictive current, too strong. Seven months ago, Sarah let go, lost in the deep.

I had her all wrong all along. She wasn't me. She never needed flesh; she needed the feathers I could once so easily imagine. I wish I could have given them to her. Her wings were so tired.

I wish I had washed her feet.

What I Knew

Marion Dane Bauer

I always knew. Knew in so deep a way that I never thought about it until, well into middle age, I found myself recoiling internally when a friend who was a massage therapist described her career as *body work.*

Surely that word, *body,* wasn't to be used in polite society!

The recoil was so deep and so instinctive that I was forced to think. What other word was there, after all? And what was wrong with bodies?

With *my* body?

Which, of course, tumbled me right back to childhood.

I was born in the Midwest in 1938 to parents of English heritage. (Watching *The Crown,* I understood perfectly the Queen's emotional distance, her total lack of curiosity about her own psyche, her prissiness.) In my family, bodies were entirely beyond mention. Certainly there were no names for intimate body parts. Except for the word "bottom," which referred only to something that could be sat upon . . . or spanked.

I grew up, in fact, with so much about my body unspoken, unacknowledged that I absorbed modesty—let's call it by its real name, *body shame*—along with the air I breathed.

None of that was unusual for girls of my generation, though certainly my mother's English reserve solidified the Puritanical rigidity of the time.

But then came the complicating factor.

My father.

My father both absorbed the everything-about-bodies-is-obscene culture from his earliest days and combined it with an obsession about all things sexual. There was hardly a topic that couldn't be turned to sex.

A leering, shame-faced sex.

If anyone mentioned a cow, he brought the bull into the conversation.

When my brother was a very little boy, Dad insisted that our mother quit hugging and kissing him. Such loving physical contact between a mother and son was . . . well, so conspicuously beyond the pale that no reason needed to be given!

That mother whom Dad called "Mommy," too, belonged exclusively to him. And he let us know that, again and again.

One of my clearest memories from being very small was getting sick during the night and climbing from my crib to make my way to my parents' bedroom. I stood far back from the closed door to call my mother. When Daddy was in there, I was forbidden. No matter the need.

(I don't remember whether she came—I assume she did—only the frightened, lonely calling.)

I also remember my father reaching inside my mother's clothes as she stood in the kitchen, fondling her breasts, exploring beneath her skirt, all the while looking over her shoulder to laugh at the disgust registering in his adolescent daughter's face.

From my father I learned that female bodies were meant to be possessed.

From my mother, from the way she stood, silent and patient while his hands roamed, from the way she seemed to accept everything about him, I learned that he was right.

My family physician/godfather completed my training by announcing one day when I was alone with him in his office that there was some light missing in me. He told me he was going to fix it.

And he went about doing that. Repeatedly.

My father's point proven.

For all of the careful repression I had learned from my mother, for all of the leering shame I had hated in my father, for all the resentment I felt toward my family doctor, my unease with the intimate workings of my body failed to protect me from predators.

It was as though I carried a sign, "Victim in Waiting."

And certainly, the fact that the occasional man in authority *wanted* my body did nothing to make me want it, too.

Or like it.

Or value it.

Or find pleasure in it.

I married nonetheless, bore children, and settled into the work I had long known was mine. Writing for children.

Why children? Probably because my mother idealized, almost idolized, her own childhood. In fact, she had worked very hard to keep me dependent and young so she could relive through me all she had loved. Thus childhood felt important to me in a way the adult world never had.

But there was another reason, too. One less easy to acknowledge.

Perhaps I chose children for my audience to avoid writing about sex. To keep the father slathering in my mind from peering over my shoulder as the words poured out.

And yet, even if that last is true, the very first novel I wrote—published as my second but the first I stumbled through—was about a foster child, a girl, and a molesting foster father.

I had foster children of my own at the time I wrote that story, and I was filled with fury over the sexual exploitation too many girls encounter in that system. It was my conscious fury that propelled the story, but it took me years to recognize who the girl really was.

After all, my own father had never touched me. Certainly not sexually. Rarely at all. But incest lived so heavily in the air I breathed every day and night of my childhood, unspoken incest, unconsummated incest, that it was the first topic I had to expunge. After that, I could settle into work . . . without any mention of sex.

In the meantime, I was finding marriage hard. It was, of course, something I was "meant" to do. And whatever I was meant to do, I set out— with clenched jaw, if necessary—to do well. Until one day I realized that I couldn't any longer.

I simply could not.

And that's when I finally let myself know the something I truly was meant to do. To be. Something that had been inside me all along, whispering in my ear, tugging at me, trying to get my attention.

Promising joy.

A joy even my too long-ignored body could recognize.

I discovered that in loving another body, touching that body, taking pleasure in it, I could learn to love, to touch, to take pleasure in my own.

If only that other body was a woman's like mine.

I was forty-seven when I came to this understanding. I thought myself the stupidest woman on Earth, that anything so fundamental, so *right,* could be hidden from me for so long.

Perhaps the discovery had waited for my father to die, for that prurient leer to be gone from the Earth. Certainly it had waited for my children to be grown. And for my writing career to be well enough established that I had a chance—just a bare chance—of surviving in the world on my own.

And so, finally, belatedly, rejoicing in my new self, I moved into adulthood.

I broke out of the mold my society had prepared for me and discovered that I could live in delight with another body, another mind, another lived experience like my own.

Today, when I climb into bed with the woman I have loved for a very long time, when I snug into her softness, her warmth, her deep acceptance, I am truly home.

And as I grow old, as senses and limbs and viscera fail, I love this flesh I was born into in a way I never knew could be possible.

I have even come to love the word.

BODY!

Yellow Towels and White Tubs

Jennifer Fischer

When I was six, I slept in the bathtub all summer. Not the beige tub in the kids' bathroom, but the white clawfoot tub filled with stuffed animals that sat in the corner of my bedroom. We traveled to Missouri that June, but a monster found me in the guest bed and haunted my nightmares back at home. So I slept in the white tub and hid beneath Pooh, Panda, and Care Bears, as well as a fluffy dog that was my mom's when she was a little girl.

Her mother was cold, rarely offered warm embraces, so my mom took comfort in a stuffed yellow dog instead. She hoped her mother's embraces would be there for the grandkids. They weren't.

In fact, the only time my grandmother Ethel and I embraced was when I helped her out of a white tub of her own, late in her life. I wrapped my arms around her as I placed a soft yellow towel around her bony shoulders.

Despite Ethel's coldness, my mother couldn't bear to let Ethel be completely cared for by strangers. So, my mom and I took turns visiting. In truth, those strangers knew my grandmother better than I did.

At the bathtub that night, I carefully washed Ethel's frail body, tending it as I would a baby bird. Her back was hunched, the result of severe osteoporosis, which my mother was diagnosed with in her 50s. Once three inches taller than me, I tower over her now.

Ethel's chest, though, was flat, like her back should have been. In 1978, to rid her body of cancer, a surgeon cut off both of her breasts. For most of my life, I never knew this. I was a baby when it happened; nobody talked about it. It seemed unimportant, insignificant. I only discovered it that night in the bathtub as I pushed a yellow washcloth across her scars.

§

Decades later, I recline in a different white tub, filled with Epsom salt and lavender oil, and push a yellow washcloth across the only surgical scar I have. It sits millimeters above my pubic hair. In the ten years following my second son's birth, it will become a source of increasing pain, though I don't know this yet. At first, the pain is a mystery.

I first mention it to a doctor when my youngest is two years old. The doctor assures me that the pain will pass, that it is "normal" for sex to be painful after childbirth. She tells me we're simply "out of practice."

I think of the varsity basketball coach in my small Texas town whose mantra was "no pain, no gain," who went to prison for four years for sexual misconduct with a minor, who sent an 18-year-old to college with no cartilage left in her knee.

My copper IUD is removed when my second son is nine. My intense menstrual pain eases, but pain during sex (or sex during pain as I've come to think of it) remains. My new doctor hoped removing the IUD would help. When it doesn't, she blames perimenopause and dryness, recommends KY Jelly and *more* sex. "Play through the pain" remains the mantra, but the pain keeps escalating. It moves out of the realm of sex and into my daily life. Running, always meditative for me, becomes unbearable. Some days, I can barely walk.

My sister connects me with Julia, a homeopath in Germany who tells me it doesn't have to be this way. Childbirth, she stresses, does not mean a postpartum life of pain. No one has told me this before. Julia is Step B in my healing process. Step A was a small camera inserted into my vagina, revealing a prolapsed uterus. Julia explains that my uterus is constantly pulling at scar adhesions from two c-sections, causing the unbearable pain I've been experiencing. The pulling is most extreme during sex and high impact sports, like running. I sob, grateful for some answers and an ally.

Steps C through Z, as far as I can tell, involve a wide variety of exercises and therapeutic processes. During my intake with a pelvic floor physical therapist, I cry again. Ten years of medical gaslighting coming to a close. No more "play through the pain" mantras. The therapist, instead, insists that my pain is unacceptable. *My* baseline is to have sex with *minimal* pain. I had given up on ever running again. My therapist, whose last name is Lavender and is vegan like my youngest son, has a different baseline: running again, pleasurable sex, a whole, full life. She is kind as she helps me navigate a complicated process: biofeedback, a pelvic wand, hip exercises, pelvic floor bracing, c-section scar massage, warm and soothing baths, etc., etc.

The handout for c-section massage that she gives me lays out three stages. Stage 1, it says, "can begin after your 6-week checkup." I am only 11 years and 39 days late.

The massage is best performed after a warm bath. Wrapped in my yellow towel, I gently rub calendula oil on and around my scar, feeling for the adhesions, which I imagine as forgotten spaghetti noodles wound together due to inattention. I encourage the noodles to let go, to release, to stretch.

Over time, the baseline pain I've become accustomed to is visible again because it's finally gone. In my daily life, I am pain free. On a good week, I run a mile.

Still, sex remains painful, though the pain is less severe. That fix is more challenging, not exclusively physical. I am learning that women who are sexual assault survivors have higher rates of birth trauma. My first c-section was rushed, an emergency, the baby likely to die if he was not removed from my uterus quickly; my body failing me, only 5 centimeters dilated. The second c-section was all about money, liability. I was on poor people's insurance and, thus, did not qualify for a VBAC. Webster tells me that birth trauma is "stress experienced by a mother during or after childbirth." I definitely qualify.

So, it is not only my "wandering womb," as the Ancient Greeks once called the uterus, that is the problem. Sex is also painful because I am terrified. To Lavender it is obvious: I am always bracing, anticipating pain, my vaginal walls tight, prepared for the pain I assume will always come. The deepest scars are psychological and can't be soothed by Epsom salt in a hot bath, but I try anyway.

I lie in my white tub, knees cradled in my hands, take a deep breath and whisper, "you are safe." With my next prescribed stretch, which is one knee only, I tell myself, "you are loved." I switch to the other knee and continue, "you deserve to *be* loved."

During the final stretch, where the base of my feet touch each other and my legs splay open, I complete my new mantra. "You deserve to feel passion, to feel pleasure, to be free of pain. You are safe and loved. You are safe and loved."

I repeat the cycle two more times before I step out of the white tub and wrap myself in the warm embrace of a soft, yellow towel, grateful for strong bones and the opportunity to finally heal.

Shame Less

Deirdre Fagan

Shame creates secrets. My siblings and I were bound together by a particular shame.

Before I was old enough to store clear memories, something went wrong in my parents' marriage and with my eldest brother. Before our parents separated and I went to live with my mother at the age of nine, there are memories of being under covers and of smells and images that I can't hold steady but I now know were instigated by our eldest brother, the one three years older than my middle brother and six years older than me.

In the heteronormative world I lived in as a kid and adolescent, I assumed that as the girl, I had been the sole target. But in our late twenties, when my middle brother and I were trying to understand why our eldest brother took his own life at twenty-five, my remaining brother and I talked for the first time about what had happened. He shared that he too had been subjected to sexually, physically, and emotionally traumatizing manipulations by our eldest brother, and that the abuse continued long after I was gone. Incest brought a combination of complex physical feelings to us both, including embarrassment, arousal, fear, guilt, shame, and compliance.

An acquired tendency to acquiesce, an understanding of arousal, and a history of keeping secrets are part of what I now suspect made me a vulnerable and willing target for a thirty-one-year-old pedophile when I was thirteen. His teeth got so deep into me as he manipulated my mind and emotions, and my mother's and her boyfriend's and all those surrounding me, that when he offered to have me move in with him at age fifteen for a "better life," because after the divorce we were poor, unstable, and always moving, I and everyone around me fell for it. That pedophile befriended and seduced confessions out of me. He said he needed to protect me. He said he needed to rescue me. My parents were neglectful. My brothers were creeps. They had all failed me.

The predator seemed true. He said he was in love with me, and I thought, for a brief time, maybe I was in love for the first time too, having never had a boyfriend before. I had had my first date at the end of eighth grade. That boy and I briefly kissed on the junior high steps during a school carnival before his mother picked us up in her station wagon. My family and I met the predator a few months later.

My body had been sexualized for as long as I had memories, which is why when I first read Nabokov's *Lolita* at 22, I was not only convinced there was such a thing as a "nymphet," but also that I had always been one, and that the pedophile had been my Humbert. For years I was haunted by these secret sexual acts that I pushed deep into my being. I had by then spent the first two decades of my life and much of my energy trying to hide the guilt and shame of these truths from others. It was exhausting.

The first person I told about the predator was my first husband. He barely reacted; he had his own scarred past. We met four months after my mother died and married six months later. I was twenty-four. I now know my secrets were partly to protect my mother and that her death signaled the first stirrings of my desire to tell. Ten months later, near the end of that brief marriage, I began therapy. The therapist helped me to understand the truth about my life with the predator and to begin telling others, including my father and brother. My father, middle brother, and I began healing talks, but my brother and I had not yet talked about the incest.

I spent the better part of my mid-twenties telling everyone who would listen about the pedophile. I wanted to shout about the abuse as loudly as possible. I wanted to tell the secrets that I had kept so long under the guise of the pedophile being my guardian. The vessel that had carried those secrets slowly began to thrive. But I was still not telling everyone all.

Before my second marriage, I confessed the darkest and most shameful secret to my husband: there had not only been an adult predator, but sibling predators too. He did not flee. He loved me for my mind, not my body, so much so that our marriage was, for a reason I would never fully understand, sexless. At the time, it felt like the purest of any relationship I had had, and it was during that embrace that I truly began to heal. I grew, but the marriage ended when I realized I still wanted and needed to be sexually desired.

Late one night, shortly after I met Bob and after making love, I told him all the abuse truths, hoping he would love me anyway. I explained that I was the victim of sexual abuse in my family and of a pedophile. Sexual interactions with the pedophile began almost a year after we met and ended a few years later, probably because I got too old. The abuse in my family and with the predator was as much emotional, perhaps more so, as physical. I continued to live with the predator until I was twenty; I had nowhere else to go.

Bob listened intently as I shared all the truths I would intellectually but emotionally never completely believe were not my fault. He cradled me in his arms and told me he was so proud of who I had become. He said he admired my strength, resilience, and ability to continue to love. So many people who had survived would shut down, he said. It was my open heart that made me all the more beautiful to him. Bob became my third husband.

My middle brother and I shared no recollection of innocence, and while my eldest brother and mother were gone before these shames of our childhood were ever openly discussed between my father, remaining brother, and me, we all understood all three of us children bore the scars of sexual trauma.

A child does not abuse without being abused. While we never determined who victimized our eldest brother, my middle brother and I were certain his and our abuse contributed to his suicide. My middle brother was perpetually tormented by his own incest memories both as victim and as perpetrator. A little more than a decade after our open conversations began, he died of alcoholism.

When we are taught early that our bodies ought to succumb to the wills of others, we are likely to conflate love and sex and be confused about our own needs and desires. Understanding and telling truths helped me to develop a keen ability to recognize threat in those I meet and to break the toxic, devastating cycle.

While my body has memories both conscious and subconscious that will remain, it now belongs only to me.

Shattering the Dark Silence

Sarita Sidhu

Mum and Dad met for the first time on their arranged wedding day, in Punjab, India, in 1959. Mum was sixteen and a half, Dad was twenty-five. Mum said when it was time to find husbands for us, the age gap had to be small.

Punjab was the epicenter of the bloody partition of India into India and Pakistan in 1947, when the hard-fought independence from Britain was finally gained. My grandfather's fabric and tailoring business became unviable when his Muslim clients could no longer pay their debts. As school was no longer affordable, my dad enlisted as a boy soldier in the Indian Army at the age of fifteen. Four and a half years later, in 1954, he joined the Merchant Navy. Here, he traveled the globe via the boiling boiler rooms of different ships.

By the time I was born at home in a Punjabi village in 1963, I already had an older sister, by eighteen months; Dad had arrived in provincial England three months earlier, in response to the labor shortages in the factories. Although the government welcomed those it had formerly colonized, the general public was less enthusiastic. Dad lived with fourteen other Indians in a house owned by one of his Indian friends, because white people refused to rent their properties to the darker-skinned émigrés from Commonwealth countries. They did shiftwork as laborers on construction sites and took shifts sleeping in the limited number of beds.

In 1964 one of Dad's Merchant Navy friends, who had talked himself into getting hired at Goodyear Tire & Rubber Company, convinced his manager to take a chance on my dad, too, who had an equally impressive work ethic. Dad was soon able to move into a house shared by fewer people. He worked for Goodyear as a laborer for twenty-two years, until he was made redundant.

When Mum arrived at this house in England with me and my older sister in 1964, she complained to Dad that it was too cold and draughty for young children; I had been so sick prior to boarding the flight over that one of the relatives had told Mum she should just throw me away if I didn't make it, before disembarking.

In 1965 Dad borrowed money from a friend to buy a house with three other friends. Dad took in one of Mum's relatives so he could save money to start a business. When I married, we bought much of my trousseau at his wildly successful store. At a discount. Which could have been bigger.

In England Mum gave birth to two more daughters. Four girls who needed dowries for their marriages, and on whom family honour, *izzath*, rested. Zero boys for whom dowries were not a prerequisite for marriage, who would have lived with them and taken care of them as they aged. Mum's sweat shop sewing on an industrial machine at home supplemented the family income. She was so skilled in her craft that she was regularly asked to stitch the samples for each line of outerwear.

My maternal grandmother had died when Mum was only six years old. The step mother beat Mum and her two siblings. Mum still has a visible scar on her forehead, left by a pan thrown at her by her stepmother. Mum vowed she would never hit her children.

When I was five years old I slept in a bed that touched wallpaper dad had meticulously applied, to create a contiguous pattern throughout the room. Some nights I swept my little fingers over the paper in search of edges, which I could scratch with my fingernail, in order to liberate pieces I could then grab between my fingertips, and pull off. And eat. I was oblivious to the damage I was doing to the décor, until Dad discovered my nocturnal obsession. Mum revealed recently that on one occasion Dad beat me so hard she was worried he'd kill me. She didn't talk to him for several days.

Every Christmas, Goodyear invited its employees to bring their children for photographs with Santa. We could also choose a gift for ourselves. One year I picked a cash register with plastic money.

When we were young, we played games where we pretended to be schoolteachers and shopkeepers. I also remember riding on my younger sister's bare back, as though she were a horse, without underwear, and enjoying the sensations I experienced.

Dad made us learn the multiplication tables each week, in consecutive order, and he tested us on random products from the cumulative tables we'd memorized. If we could answer everything correctly, we were allowed to go outside and play. My older sister rarely made it outside. Mrs. Jones wrote that I had some way to go before my English was as good as my mathematics.

As a six- or seven-year-old girl I sat in Mrs. Jones's classroom with the metal table leg between mine, to feel pressure against my vagina.

I wonder if Mum had ever voiced her disapproval when Dad placed us on top of himself, in their bed, when we took the daytime naps he mandated.

"Why were you bloodsuckers all born into our house?" became a familiar rhetorical question after one of us had behaved inappropriately. For example, at ten, my older sister had set her hair free, had her white school shirt unbuttoned too far down, skirt pulled up too high, and worn makeup to school. Dad called her a witch and beat her with a leather whip. Probably to teach us all a lesson. He told us to spit on her. We did. At seventeen she left home during the night with her divorced white teacher and Dad said she was dead to him. Mum took my younger sister to India when she was fourteen because "She was also bringing shame upon the family." For the most part, I escaped into my schoolbooks and enjoyed the praise I received when I excelled.

No one had ever called Dad out when he regularly sat with an object—a cushion, a baby's feet wrapped into a blanket—pressing into his genitalia, while he fidgeted around, talking with the visitors.

Mum rarely shared family secrets but she confided in me a few years ago that Dad's sister in India had had a child out of wedlock. She said that Dad was pushed forward by his three older brothers to break the news to my aunt—the youngest of six siblings—that they were arranging her marriage; one of the conditions was that she give up her child first. She cried and screamed and cursed Dad. Through the years Mum often criticized my aunt for being bitter and mean spirited. I wondered if she became that way after marriage.

Mum also said recently that Dad had never given love. And he had never received it.

When I finally moved out of my in-laws' house, after five and a half years of marriage, I had the privacy to reconnect with my older sister. We shared our experiences with Dad. When Dad began to ask my two-year-old daughter if she wanted to sleep with him, I quickly retorted that she did not.

A few days later I picked up the phone receiver with a shaking hand, my heart beating wildly, deafeningly, and dialed my parents' number. Dad answered, and I blurted "I know what you did!" Clearly he was as shocked as I was, and he just kept saying "What are you talking about? What did I do? Tell me what I did!" I shouted back at him "You know what you did! You know what you did when we were little!" After we had gone around in a couple of circles, I said I was going, and I replaced the receiver.

I sat on the stairs, my head in my still-shaking hands, and cried. I was certain they wouldn't want to see me ever again either.

Everyone in the family took Dad's side against me and my older sister. He said we were too westernized. He had always been the victim, even after beating us; he often sat down, exhausted, and told Mum to bring him water.

To maintain their relationship with my in-laws, my parents attended my younger daughter's birthday celebration. After everyone had left to go home, Mum said she had a cousin in India who often crept into the bed she shared with her older sister. Her sister made such a noise in the dark silence, asking him loudly what he was doing, he had no choice but to leave. Mum continued to defend Dad. My aunt died in her thirties. I never met her.

We cannot change where we come from. But we can interrogate the constructs that maintain the status quo and identify the beneficiaries of these prisons. When we return Shhhame to its rightful owners, it can no longer silence us, disempower us. Speaking out is a revolutionary act. This is the path to liberation. This is how hope blooms.

The Question Body

Maureen Aitken

What if your body is glorious now, and you are about to miss it for the ritual of beating yourself with a scale?

What if the days when you stomped your feet to look tough actually did protect you?

What if you didn't blame yourself for what you called bad days, decisions, diets, failures?

What if, instead, you saw it as unfinished business that needed to show up and pass through?

What if hiding was the best you could do at the time?

What if the years you were tormented by him, the years he called you porker, were really about his belief that he was better than everyone else?

What if your tears were your heart's thunderstorm? Lightning strikes imploding judgment? Hard rains quenching the neglected cracking lands where wonder once bore secret fruit?

What if you put down the idea that replaying cruel phrases in your mind would make you stronger?

What if you listened to the girl whispering in the corner of your being when she said, "All I ever wanted was for you to love me. Tell me, why is that so hard?"

What if you did that, loved the one part of you that truly belonged?

Contributors

Camille U. Adams is a writer from Trinidad and Tobago. She earned her MFA in Poetry from CUNY and is a current Ph.D. Candidate in Creative Nonfiction. Having been awarded the sole full scholarship for *Granta Magazine*'s inaugural nature writing course, Camille's currently working on narrative pieces to join those featured in *Passages North, Citron Review, XRAY Literary Magazine, Variant Literature, The Forge Literary Magazine, Kweli Magazine,* and elsewhere. Camille is also a nonfiction editor at *The Account Magazine, Variant Literature,* and a memoir reader for *Split Lip Magazine.* She's querying her first memoir while at work on her second.

Maureen Aitken's short-story collection, *The Patron Saint of Lost Girls,* won the Nilsen Prize, the top *Foreword Review* INDIE Gold Prize for General Fiction, and ranked in the Kirkus Best Indie Books of 2019. Her collection received a Kirkus Star, a Foreword Star, and was a Finalist for the Minnesota Book Award. Two of her stories were nominated for a Pushcart Prize. Maureen's short stories have been published in numerous journals, including *The Missouri Review, Prairie Schooner, New Letters,* and the international anthology, *The Bering Strait and Other Stories. Emerge Literary* recently nominated her piece, "Sunflowers" for Best Microfiction.

Kathryn Aldridge-Morris is a writer living in Bristol, UK. Her work appears in *Wigleaf* Top 50, *Pithead Chapel, New Flash Fiction Review, Flash Frog, Ellipsis Zine, Emerge Literary Journal, South Florida Poetry Journal, Stanchion* and elsewhere. She has won Manchester School of Writing's *QuietManDave* prize and the flash fiction contest organised by Welsh publisher, *Lucent Dreaming,* and her stories have been nominated for Best Microfiction and the Pushcart Prize. You can read her flash narratives and poems at <u>www.kamwords.com</u>. She tweets @kazbarwrites.

Melissa Flores Anderson is a Latinx Californian and an award-winning journalist who lives in her hometown with her young son and husband. A

2023 Best of the Net nominee for CNF, her creative work has been published in more than two dozen journals or anthologies, and she is a reader/editor with *Roi Fainéant Press.* She has co-authored a novelette, "Roadkill," that is forthcoming with *Emerge Literary Journal.* Follow her on Twitter and Bluesky @melissacuisine or IG/Threads @theirishmonths. Read her work at melissafloresandersonwrites.com.

Andrew Baise is an engineer by trade, an avid calorie counter, and a novice outdoorsman with a lifelong appreciation for writing.

Eleonora Balsano's short fiction has won, has been placed or listed in several international competitions, such as the the Bridport Prize, and is featured in literary magazines and anthologies in the UK and the US. She is a reader for *Longleaf Review* and *West Word.* Eleonora lives in Brussels and is working on a dystopian novel. You can follow her on Twitter @norami.

Marion Dane Bauer is the author of more than 100 books for young people, ranging from picture books to young adult novels, fiction and nonfiction.

G. Lev Baumel is a mother, writer, teacher, and polyglot. Most of the time, her body resides in California, though she has left pieces of herself in Brooklyn, Antwerp, El Salvador and all the other parts of the world that created and shaped her. She writes under a pseudonym to honor those who came before. G.'s limited edition collage book, *The Disappearing Man,* will be available in December 2023. You can visit her virtually at: glevbaumelwriter

DeAnna Beachley is a teacher, historian, poet, and essayist. Her poetry has appeared in *Red Rock Review, Sandstone & Silver, Thimble, The Ekphrastic Review Challenge, Slant, Blue Earth Review, Gyroscope, Anatomy of an Essay, The Book of Life After Death,* and forthcoming in one other anthology. When not teaching or writing, she enjoys hiking and bird watching.

Kelli Short Borges writes essays, short stories, and flash fiction from her home in Phoenix, Arizona. Her work appears in *Gone Lawn, MoonPark Review, The*

Tahoma Literary Review, The Sunlight Press, SoFloPoJo, The Citron Review, Ghost Parachute, Flash Boulevard, FlashFlood Journal, multiple anthologies, and elsewhere. Kelli is a 2022 Best of the Net and 2023 Best Microfiction nominee. She is currently working on her first novel.

Barb Mayes Boustead is a meteorologist, climatologist, instructor, and writer living with her partner and child near Omaha, Nebraska.

Melissa Llanes Brownlee (she/her), a native Hawaiian writer living in Japan, has work published and forthcoming in *The Rumpus, Fractured Lit, Flash Frog, Gigantic Sequins, Cream City Review, Cincinnati Review* miCRo, and *Craft,* and honored in *Best Small Fictions, Best Microfictions,* and *Wigleaf* Top 50. Read *Hard Skin* from Juventud Press and *Kahi and Lua* from Alien Buddha. She tweets @lumchanmfa and talks story melissallanesbrownlee.com.

Amy Champeau is a Jungian psychoanalyst, somatic psychotherapist and spiritual director in St Louis Park, MN. Her work explores the intersections between trauma, the body, and spiritual development. Her work has been published in *Tiferet Journal, Pilgrimage,* and *Persimmon Tree,* and her essay, *Naming,* was long-listed for *Prism*'s Creative Nonfiction Award. In her spare time she enjoys contra dancing and hanging out with her five teenage grandkids.

Ezekiel Cork is a trans writer who lives in Missoula, Montana with his wife and two rescue mutts. He runs and hikes the local trails, loves cookies, coffee and trucker hats. His writing has been published in *Bending Genres, X-RAY Lit, Pidgeonholes, Savant Garde* and others. His work has been nominated for Best of the Net and he was a finalist in the last *Glimmer Train* Short Story competition.

Jocelyn Jane Cox lives in the Hudson Valley of New York with her husband and son. She writes creative nonfiction, essays, fiction, and humor.

Aria Dominguez (she/they) is a writer whose poetry and creative nonfiction navigate the terrain between beauty and pain. Her work has been nominated for Best of the Net and the Pushcart Prize, and she was winner of the 2021 Porch Prize in Creative Nonfiction, a Fall 2021 Brooklyn Poets Fellowship, the 2022 *Sunlight Press* Essay Contest, and a 2023 Money for Women Nonfiction Award. Aria works with a nonprofit focused on food justice and lives in Saint Paul with her son.

Jacqueline Doyle's award-winning flash fiction chapbook *The Missing Girl* is available from *Black Lawrence Press*. She has recent creative nonfiction in *The Gettysburg Review, Passages North, Fourth Genre* and *EPOCH*. Her work has been featured in *Creative Nonfiction*'s "Sunday Short Reads" and has earned nine Notable Essay citations in *Best American Essays*. She lives in the San Francisco Bay Area.

Deirdre Fagan is the award-winning author of a poetry collection, *Phantom Limbs* (2023), a memoir *Find a Place for Me: Embracing Love and Life in the Face of Death (2022),* a short story collection, *The Grief Eater (2020),* a chapbook of poetry, *Have Love (2019), and a reference book, Critical Companion to Robert Frost (2007).* She is a widow, wife, mother of two and professor and coordinator of creative writing at Ferris State University.

Jennifer Fischer is a writer, mediamaker, and teaching artist whose work has been featured by NBCLatino, ABC, Univision, Fusion, NBCBLK, etc. Her film "THE wHOLE" premiered at Amnesty International's 50th Anniversary Human Rights Conference. Recent publications include pieces in *Ms. Magazine, Last Girls Club, Literary Mama, Oranges Journal, Barzakh Magazine* and *Under Her Eye* from *Black Spot Books*. An essay of hers appears in *What is a Criminal? Answers from Inside the U.S. Justice System*, an anthology from *Routledge*, published Jan. 2023.

Elizabeth Fletcher is a writer and yoga therapist from Saint Paul, Minnesota. Her fiction and nonfiction have appeared in *New Flash Fiction Review,*

Lost Balloon, The Leaping Clear, Tiferet and elsewhere. She is an assistant nonfiction editor for *Pithead Chapel*. She facilitates an Embodied Writing practice online and offers workshops that bridge movement and writing. Connect with her on Twitter @esfletcher or on her website www.esfletcher. com.

Jennifer Fliss (she/her) is the writer of the story collections *As If She Had a Say* (2023) and *The Predatory Animal Ball* (2021.) Her writing has appeared in *F(r)iction, The Rumpus, The Washington Post*, and elsewhere. She can be found on Twitter at @writesforlife or via her website, www.jenniferflisscreative.com.

Melody Greenfield has an MFA in creative nonfiction writing from Antioch University Los Angeles. She has been published in *Brevity, The Los Angeles Review*, the *Los Angeles Review of Books, The Manifest-Station, Sledgehammer Lit*, the J*ewish Literary Journal, Longridge Review, The RavensPerch*, and elsewhere, with work forthcoming in *Hippocampus Magazine*. She has been nominated for Best Small Fiction award by *Meow Meow Pow Pow* and Best of the Net by *Kelp Journal*. Melody and her Canadian husband (both Team Dark Chocolate) live in LA, where she teaches and blogs about Pilates, and he teaches elementary school.

Suzanne Hicks is a disabled writer living with multiple sclerosis. Her stories have appeared in *Maudlin House, Roi Fainéant, New Flash Fiction Review, MicroLit Almanac,* and elsewhere. She lives in Las Vegas, Nevada with her husband and their animals. Read more at suzannehickswrites.com.

Ann Kathryn Kelly writes from New Hampshire's Seacoast region. She's an editor with *Barren Magazine*, a columnist with *WOW! Women on Writing*, and she works in the technology sector. Ann leads writing workshops for a nonprofit that offers therapeutic arts programming to people living with brain injury. Her writing has appeared in a number of literary journals. https://annkkelly.com/

Jesse Lee Kercheval is a writer, poet, translator and artist. Her latest books include the poetry collections *I Want To Tell You* (University of Pittsburgh Press) and *Un pez dorado no te sirve para nada / A Goldfish Buys You Nothing* (Editorial Yaugarú). She is the author of the memoir *Space* (University of Wisconsin Press) which won an Alex Award from the American Library Association. Her graphic memoir, *French Girl,* is forthcoming from Fieldmouse Press.

Amanda Leigh Lichtenstein is a writer and editor whose writing has appeared in *Teachers & Writers Magazine, CNN, NPR, Al Jazeera, Hypertext, Another Chicago Magazine* and *Contrary,* among others. Poems appear in *Horseless Review, La Petite Zine, Painted Bride Quarterly and Punch Drunk Press* and *Fortunate Traveler,* among others. After nearly a decade based on the East African islands of Zanzibar (Unguja), Amanda is now rooted back in her hometown of Skokie, Illinois, where she works as an editor and reporter with *The World,* a global news radio program.

Nina B. Lichtenstein, is a native of Oslo, Norway. She holds a PhD in French literature from UCONN and an MFA in creative nonfiction from University of Southern Maine. Her essays have appeared in *The WaPo, Lilith, Full Grown People, Tablet Magazine, Dorothy Parker's Ashes*, and *AARP's "The Ethel,"* among other places, and in two anthologies, *Ink* (*Hippocampus Books,* 2022) and *Stained: Writing About Menstruation* (*Querencia Press,* 2023). Nina's memoir "Body: My Life in Parts" is looking for a home. She lives in Maine where her kayak, bike, and nature trails help keep her sane.

Tracy Rothschild Lynch holds an MA from VCU and an MFA from Queens University, Charlotte. She adores teaching all ages, particularly emerging writers as they build confidence and stock toolkits. In addition to online courses and private coaching, Tracy teaches at the Virginia Museum of Fine Arts. Her essay, "When Organ Becomes Metaphor," recently placed second in the annual Lit/South Awards. A previous Pushcart finalist, Tracy's been published in *Pithead Chapel, Cleaver, (mic)ro(mac), Epoch Press*(Scotland),

Brain,Child, Janus Literary, and others. A firm believer in the *body + words = healing* equation, she's honored to appear in this beautiful anthology.

Alison McGhee is the #1 NY Times bestselling writer of novels, poems, essays, and picture books for all ages, including *Someday, Never Coming Back*, and *What I Leave Behind*. She is the recipient of many awards, including the Geisel Medal, the Christopher Award, four Minnesota Book Awards, two state arts board grants, and a McKnight Fellowship. Her work has been translated into more than twenty languages.

Claudia Monpere's creative nonfiction appears in *River Teeth, Creative Nonfiction Sunday Reads, The Forge, Smokelong Quarterly* and several anthologies. Her short stories, flash fiction and poetry appear in many literary magazines, including *The Kenyon Review, The Cincinnati Review, New Ohio Review, Trampset, Smokelong Quarterly, Fictive Dream* and *Ghost Parachute*. She is the recipient of a Hedgebrook Residency and *The Georgetown Review* Fiction Award and was shortlisted for *The Smokey* 2022. She tweets @ ClaudiaMonpere.

James Montgomery is a flash fiction writer based in Staffordshire, UK. He has won the Pokrass Prize and Retreat West's best micro fiction prize, and been highly commended in the Bath Flash Fiction Award. James' stories have been published in various anthologies and literary magazines, including *Reflex Fiction, Maudlin House, Gone Lawn, Janus Literary, Ellipsis Zine, Twin Pies Literary* and elsewhere, and he has been nominated for the Pushcart Prize and Best of the Net.

Ellen Birkett Morris's novel *Beware the Tall Grass* is the winner of the Donald L. Jordan Award for Literary Excellence, judged by Lan Samantha Chang, and will be published in 2024 by *CSU Press*. She is the author of *Lost Girls: Short Stories*, winner of the Pencraft Award and finalist for the Clara Johnson, IAN and Best Book awards. Her essays have appeared in *Newsweek, AARP's The Ethel, Oh Reader* magazine, and on *National Public Radio*.

Sandell Morse is the prize-winning author of the memoir *The Spiral Shell, A French Village Reveals Its Secrets of Jewish Resistance in World War II.* Morse's nonfiction has been noted in *The Best American Essays* series and published in *Creative Nonfiction, Ploughshares,* the *New England Review, Fourth Genre ASCENT, Solstice,* and *Tiferet* among others. She lives in New Hampshire with Zeus, her Standard Poodle.

Monica Nathan is a Pushcart-nominated writer whose work has appeared in *The Fiddlehead, Barren Magazine, The Feathertale Review,* and other publications. Last year, she was selected as one of the most promising emerging writers by *Toronto's Diaspora Dialogues.* She is a Contributing Editor at *Barren Magazine,* an advisor for the *Festival of Literary Diversity,* and spends her time working on a novel. She lives in Toronto but home is anywhere with her husband and two kids. Find her on social media: Twitter: @monicanathan Instagram: @monicapnathan

Claude Olson (she/they) is a writer and educator currently based in Washington, DC. Born with achondroplasia, a form of dwarfism, Claude uses their experience with physical disability to advocate and uplift others in the disabled community, such as through her role as Disability Culture Coordinator at Bowdoin College. She has been previously published in *The Massachusetts Review.*

Terry Opalek resides in Chicago. He is an emerging writer working on his first memoir and is a gay man. He is an Intuitive Coach & workshop facilitator.

Melissa Ostrom is the author of *The Beloved Wild* (Feiwel & Friends, 2019), a Junior Library Guild book and an Amelia Bloomer Award selection, and *Unleaving* (Feiwel & Friends, 2019). Her stories have appeared in many journals and been selected for *Best Small Fictions 2019, Best Microfiction 2020, Best Small Fictions 2021, Best Microfiction 2021,* and *Wigleaf Top 50* 2022. She lives with her husband, children, and dog Mocha in Holley, New York. Learn more at www.melissaostrom.com or find her on Twitter @melostrom.

Maggie Pahos is a writer and teacher living in Portland, Oregon. Her work has appeared in *the Rumpus, Brevity, the Colorado Review, the Pittsburgh Post-Gazette*, and elsewhere. When she's not writing, she's hiking with her husband and their dog, Mudbug. Maggie writes the newsletter GOOD/GRIEF. To read more, visit www.maggiepahos.com.

Jane Palmer (she/they) is a professor and part-time MFA student in Washington, DC. She spends her time working toward a world without violence.

Wendy Parman is both a performer and author with a thriving voice studio in Chicago. She was recently published in the Rock 'n Roll issue of *Dorothy Parker's Ashes*, and frequently performs her original songs, stories, and personal essays. Her works include a musical memoir with a very long name, and a musical comedy on Youtube, "Callle's Solo Web Series." She's currently working on a memoir, when she isn't chasing after her newly adopted kitten, Felina Furrante.

Tania Richard is a published writer, award-winning actress, teacher, and antiracism educator. Her platform *Tania!s Take* showcases her podcast, essays, DEI educational content and videos. Her blog, *Writing My Mind* was on *The Chicago Tribune's* blog site for ten years. She's also an award-winning playwright. Her commentary can be heard on *OUT Chicago, NPR's The Story, All Things Considered* and *WTTW's Chicago Tonight*.

Kim Steutermann Rogers lives with her husband and 16-year-old dog Lulu in Hawaii. Her essay, "Following the Albatross Home" was recognized as notable in *Best American Travel Writing*. Her journalism has published in *National Geographic, Audubon,* and *Smithsonian;* and her prose in *The Citron Review, Milk Candy Review, Gone Lawn, Bending Genres, Flash Boulevard, Atticus Review, CHEAP POP, Hippocampus,* and elsewhere. She was awarded residencies at Storyknife Writers Retreat in Alaska in 2016 and 2021 and Dorland Mountain Arts in Temecula, California in 2022 and 2023. Find her on social media @kimsrogers.

Kim Ruehl is a music journalist whose work has been published by *Billboard, YES Magazine, Seattle Weekly,* and others. A former editor-in-chief of *No Depression* (the roots music journal), her book *A Singing Army: Zilphia Horton and the Highlander Folk School* was one of *NPR*'s Favorite Books of 2021. She hosts the songwriting podcast *Why We Write,* featuring in-depth discussions about songwriting with artists such as Rosanne Cash, Allison Russell, Peter Rowan, and more. She is currently working on a memoir about her experiences at the intersection of family, community, and infertility.

Lizz Schumer is the author of *Buffalo Steel* and *Biography of a Body.* She works as an editor at *Good Housekeeping* and teaches at New York University.

Sarita Sidhu is a writer and activist in Irvine, California, and a graduate from the Antioch University Los Angeles MFA in Creative Nonfiction program. She was born in India, grew up in working-class England, and moved to the US in 1999. Her work has appeared in *The Sun (Readers Write), 100 Word Story, Emerge Literary Journal, Riverside Art Museum's Online Exhibition, Lunch Ticket* and elsewhere. While taking our collective work seriously, she understands the importance of laughing and dancing in the revolution. She can be found on Instagram @saritaksid

Whitney Vale, MFA Creative Nonfiction from Ashland University. Poetry includes a chapbook, *Journey with the Ferryman (Finishing Line Press)* and poems in *Gyroscope Review: The Crone Issue, Harpy Hybrid Review, Prospectus: A Literary Offering, Autumn Sky Poetry Daily, Quartet* and *RockPaperPoem,* and the anthology *Haunted (Pork Belly Press.)* Prose in *Black Fork Review,* forthcoming in the anthologies *Awakenings, The 2023 Writer's Block Anthology,* and *The Palisades Review.* She has been a finalist for the Joy Harjo award, Barry Lopez award, and *Minerva Rising*'s memoir award.

Karen J. Weyant is a poet and essayist who lives in northern Pennsylvania.

Cynthia Wold earned her BA in Psychology at the University of Minnesota, and an MLS in the study of Love at Metropolitan State University. In 2018, Cynthia formed "Scribble River," a regular open forum for writing in community for the purpose of self-discovery. She is co-author of "The Art of Convening," and other pieces have been published in *Emerge Literary Journal* and *Haute Dish*. She is a poet and writer who wears comfortable shoes and lives with her husband in Minneapolis, MN.

Sue Zueger is a writer and middle school teacher. Her poetry and creative nonfiction have been published in *Emerge Literary Journal, Ricochet Magazine,* and the poetry anthology *The Scandalous Lives of Butterflies.* She lives in Sioux Falls, South Dakota, with her husband and a voluminous record collection.